FINDING A WAY
FORWARD
AFTER LOSS

PRAISE FOR *Finding Your Way Forward After Loss*

"I first connected with Eyum through a Maxwell Leadership coaching partnership, where her deep listening, compassion, and steady presence stood out immediately. *In Finding A Way Forward After Loss,* she combines her own profound experiences with trusted grief frameworks and a multicultural perspective to create a timely, insightful guide for anyone navigating loss or supporting someone who is. I highly recommend this meaningful work."
— Chiweni Chimbwete, PhD
CEO, Leaders DISCovery
Maxwell Leadership Team Member

"After the passing of my mother, *Finding A Way Forward After Loss* came as a timely and deeply comforting companion. It reminded me that the overwhelming emotions of grief are not signs of losing control, but a natural and necessary part of healing. Eyum's stories and her journey through loss moved me deeply. She has written something that doesn't just explain grief but sits with you in it. A powerful gift for anyone facing pain, loss, or grief."
— Sylvia Stevenson Assoc. CIPD CDE®
Director & Certified Diversity Practitioner, Absolute Diversity Ltd

"Grief can take a heavy toll when we don't know how to navigate it. This book offers both guidance and encouragement for those experiencing loss. Rich in insight and compassion, it will be a great source of comfort for anyone grieving."
— Abel Acheme
Principal Partner, Abees Global 05 Consults Ltd

"Well researched yet written in clear, accessible language, this book makes the complexities of grief easy to understand and apply. Whether you are grieving yourself or supporting someone who is, *Finding A Way Forward After Loss* is a must-read."
— **Rosemary Adole**
Education Consultant, Bee Best Christopher Academy

"This book explores the many dimensions of grief including the parts people rarely talk about. I especially valued how clearly Eyum explains how to ask for help, something many people struggle with but don't know how to begin. Finding A Way Forward After Loss helps a grieving person feel seen, restores hope, and gently encourages healing."
— **Theresa Owuna**
Consultant, Autstrip Travel Services Limited

"I deeply enjoyed reading this book. Eyum has a remarkable ability to articulate the experiences people struggle to put into words. At times I came to tears, seeing my own story and pain reflected so clearly. This book will help many."
— **Marian Favors**
Executive Director, KARL STORZ Endoscopy

"This book explains so much of what I experienced in 2024, especially the shame of a violent death, the rumours, the withdrawal. I shut myself away and struggled in silence. If I had this book then, it would have helped me immensely. Eyum's story moved me to tears, and it also helped me understand something I had never realised before—that divorce can bring grief too. Now I finally understand what I was feeling."
— **Zipporah Eje**
Principal Consultant, Zedesel Limited

FINDING A WAY FORWARD AFTER LOSS

A COMPASSIONATE AND PRACTICAL GUIDE TO HEALING AND HOPE

EYUM EJIGA

ISBN: 978-0-9574241-9-7

Email: info@ ee-bridging-solutions.co.uk
https://ee-bridging-solutions.co.uk

DEDICATION

This book is dedicated to my daughters,
Ochanya-Praise, Olijeh-Precious & Eyum-Priscilla.
We have experienced many griefs as a family,
and I am proud of the courage each of you has
shown in moving forward.

CONTENTS

ACKNOWLEDGEMENTS....................9

INTRODUCTION....................11
Is Something Wrong with Me?

CHAPTER 1 15
Am I dreaming?

CHAPTER 2 33
Why is Grief So Awful?

CHAPTER 3 47
How Do I Process Grief?

CHAPTER 4 71
How are you Coping?

CHAPTER 5 91
Why Are They So Unfair?

CHAPTER 6 107
Why Do I feel shame?

CHAPTER 7 127
Why Do I feel Guilty moving forward?

CHAPTER 8 145
Will This Pain Ever Go Away?

CHAPTER 9....................157
When Do I Need Additional Help?

CHAPTER 10....................177
How Do I Move forward With Love?

CONCLUSION 191

APPENDICES 197
NOTES...203

ACKNOWLEDGEMENTS

First and foremost, my profound appreciation goes to Almighty God for helping me not only to go through grief, but also to use my experience to help others.

A big thank you to all of you who granted me interviews and shared your grief experiences to enrich this work. Because some of you preferred that your real names not be used, I will not be mentioning them here. Your resilience in moving forward after your loss is remarkable. Many of you not only shared your stories but also took time out of your busy schedules to read the manuscript and offer valuable suggestions.

My sincere thanks to my friends, Annick Gombe and Marian Favors. You both are great examples of people who have found a way forward after experiencing unimaginable grief.

To my friend, Zipporah Eje, thank you for your professionalism in proofreading this manuscript. Having recently experienced a devastating loss yourself, I know how difficult it must have been for you to undertake this work. I also say a massive thank you to Sylvia Stevenson, Chiweni Chimbwete, Abel Acheme, Theresa Owuna, and Rosemary Adole for reading the manuscript and sharing their reflections.

Finally, to my many friends and family members whose opinions and encouragement I sought while working on this book, I say thank you. Even though I have not mentioned all your names here, I truly appreciate your support and contributions.

Introduction

IS SOMETHING WRONG WITH ME?

If you are holding this book, there is a reason. You have lost something, and the way you are responding to that loss is understandable. The confusion, the exhaustion, the heaviness, the moments when you don't feel like yourself or wonder why you cannot "handle this better" simply mean you are grieving and not that something is wrong with you.

Grief does not follow rules or timelines, and it does not arrive in a single, recognisable form. It can show up as sadness or anger, numbness or fear, guilt or longing. It can affect your body, your thoughts, your relationships, and your sense of identity. When grief lingers or changes you, it is easy to assume you are failing or broken. You are not. Nothing is wrong with you. What you are experiencing is a deeply human response to loss.

I know how powerful it is to hear those words because there were times in my own life when I needed them, too. I have known grief in many forms. I have loved and raised a child born with severe disabilities—a journey marked by devotion, exhaustion, deep uncertainty, fierce hope, and the complicated grief of caregiving. After fifteen years, I also knew the heartbreak of saying goodbye. Within a short period of time, I experienced further loss when my mother died just three months after my daughter. I have also known the grief of divorce—the loss of a shared future, the unravelling of identity, and the quiet ache of rebuilding a life when what once felt certain is gone.

These experiences did not break me, but they did reshape me. They taught me something I wish more people were told; that grief is not reserved for death of a person alone, but it accompanies endings of many kinds.

> *Healing does not mean returning to who you were but learning how to live as who you are becoming*

Through each chapter of pain, I discovered something essential; not because I was strong, but because grief required me to become honest. Honest about my limits. Honest about my need for support. Honest about the fact that healing does not mean returning to who you were but learning how to live as who you are becoming.

Along this journey, a calling also emerged. Again and again, I found myself sitting with others in their grief, people who felt lost, ashamed of their pain, or pressured to move forward before they were ready. I listened to stories spoken quietly, sometimes for the very first time. I saw how often grief was misunderstood, minimized, or rushed, and how rarely people were given permission to grieve without judgment.

What I learned is this: most people are not looking to be fixed. They are looking to be understood. This book grew out of that understanding. It was written to offer what I once needed myself, and what I have seen so many others searching for—clear language for confusing experiences, reassurance when self-doubt creeps in, and practical guidance for finding steadiness again, one moment at a time.

Grief is one of the most universal human experiences, yet many of us are unprepared when it comes. We are taught how to succeed, endure, and stay strong, but rarely how to mourn. When grief lasts longer than expected, reshapes us, or refuses to follow neat stages or timelines, we begin to wonder if something is wrong with us but there isn't.

Grief can be overwhelming, disorienting, and deeply unfair. It can affect your body, your faith, your work, your relationships, and your sense of identity. It can arrive in waves or settle in quietly, but none of these responses mean you are doing grief incorrectly. They mean you are responding to loss in the way your mind, body, and heart know how.

This book does not promise quick healing or easy answers. It will not ask you to "move on" or find meaning before you are ready. Instead, it offers something steadier and more compassionate: understanding for what you are experiencing, language for the pain that feels impossible to name, and practical guidance for finding your footing again, one step at a time.

Within these pages, you will encounter real stories, shared with care because grief needs witnesses. You will also find tools grounded in psychology, grief research, and lived experience, presented gently and without overwhelming theory, and with respect for your pace and capacity.

Healing, as I have come to understand it, does not mean forgetting or leaving your loved one behind. It means learning how to carry grief differently and discovering that life can still hold meaning, connection, and even joy, not as a betrayal of what was lost, but as a continuation of love.

You do not need to read this book in a hurry, neither do you need to read it in order. Some chapters may meet you exactly where you are; others may be for another season. Take what serves you. Leave what doesn't. Return to it when you are ready.

This book is a companion for your grief journey. And as you begin, I want you to hold this truth close:

- Nothing is wrong with you.
- You are grieving.
- And no matter where you are and how you feel right now, healing and hope are possible.

Chapter 1

AM I DREAMING?

It was the start of the school summer holidays in England in 2019. My third daughter, Eyum-Priscilla promised to make the holiday very memorable for herself and her little sister, Grace, so she planned exciting activities for each day of the holiday.

By the end of the first week, the whole family could feel the excitement as the holiday unfolded just as she had planned. On Monday they went for a day-camp meeting. On Tuesday they visited the museum. On Wednesday they went to the cinema. Thursday was spent doing fun activities at home. On Friday they had a picnic in the park. On Saturday they accompanied me to a meeting I hosted at the Crowne Plaza Hotel. And on Sunday, after church, we all attended a birthday party.

The following morning, Monday 5th August, I woke up and noticed that Grace had chest congestion and was breathing very fast. This was not unusual, as she had been prone to chest infections in the past. I decided to take her to the Emergency Unit at the Royal Berkshire Hospital in Reading to have it checked. Normally, with such chest infections, she would be nebulised and prescribed some anti-biotics, so that was what I expected to happen. We checked in at the hospital and waited to be seen. However, when it was time for the triage nurse to examine her and take her vital signs, the machine did not seem to be picking up much signal.

"This machine can sometimes be temperamental," the nurse said, as she tapped it in an attempt to make it work.

After several attempts, she called another nurse who appeared more experienced. When this second nurse examined Grace, she looked alarmed and immediately asked that she be moved to another examination area. Soon, doctors joined the nurses and began attending to her.

Then, within minutes, my daughter stopped breathing. All attempts to resuscitate her failed. Like a terrible nightmare unfolding before my eyes, my daughter slipped away right there in front of me.

The whole incident felt like a movie playing before me, and I could not believe what was happening. How could someone who was so happy and dancing in her wheelchair yesterday suddenly die like this? I wondered. Or am I dreaming?

I was in total shock.

With the help of the hospital staff, I called my two daughters, Olijeh and Eyum-Priscilla, whom I had left at home that morning, and asked them to come to the hospital.

"Mum, is everything okay?" they asked.

I could not bring myself to break the news to them over the phone. Even in their wildest imagination, they could not have thought that Grace had died that morning.

When I went to bed around ten o'clock the night before, the two of them were still watching a movie with Gracie. Since it was the holidays, there was no rush to go to bed or wake up early the next day. In fact, it was Olijeh who put her to bed that night. You can imagine their shock when they arrived at the hospital and heard the news.

My pastor, Bishop Joel Thomas, and a dear sister, Minister Gladys, also came to the hospital to support us as soon as they were called.

We had to wait a few days before breaking the news to my eldest daughter, Ochanya, who was living in America and preparing to sit for her CPA qualification exams at the time. It was also a great shock to her. The last time she saw Grace was in May that year when the family attended her graduation. It could never have occurred to her that that would be the last time she would see her little sister.

For days, I could not sleep, pray, or even cry properly because of the shock. It was only a few weeks later, when I received her death certificate, that the reality truly hit me. That was when I began to weep.

I was in deep anguish, overwhelmed with grief, not only because I had lost a child, but also because of everything I felt I had lost with her.

Grace was a very special child with special needs. She was born with some missing limbs, and her condition was diagnosed as Cornelia de Lange syndrome. Her birth brought me great distress, pain, and anxiety until the Lord took me through a process of healing. Through that journey, I found comfort and hope for both her future and mine.

That experience led me to write my first book, *He Gave Me Comfort*, where I share the full story of her birth and how God comforted me.

It took me a long time to adjust my life and learn how to care for Grace. I made many sacrifices to do so. Her condition required full-time attention, and in those early years I was her only carer. I had to give up everything to care for her. I gave up my business, my career, and many other pursuits. I even gave up the simple freedom to do what I wanted, so that I could be the mother that Gracie needed.

After fifteen long years—just when I felt that I had finally learned how to be that mother, she was taken from me.

I felt cheated, robbed, and devastated.

My deepest cry was, "Lord, why would you let me go through so much pain, sacrifice, and adjustment to care for this child, only to take her away from me?"

I dreaded her funeral. I cannot even begin to explain how I felt at the thought that my daughter would be buried in the ground.

Thankfully, I made it through that day.

A PHONE CALL FROM NIGERIA

On the 15th of November 2019, just three months after Grace passed away, I was at work when my brother, Johnson, called me from Nigeria with the devastating news that our mother had died.

"What? How can that be?" I wondered in disbelief. "Here I am still trying to heal from the death of my daughter, and now my mother is gone too?"

To say that I was devastated would be an understatement.

"How could Mama die just like that without enjoying the fruits of her labour?" I cried.

This was the deepest source of my anguish because my mother had sacrificed so much for us—her children, and for the entire family. She was a secondary school teacher who valued education greatly. When my father's financial situation deteriorated due to politics and mismanagement, she denied herself many comforts to ensure that my five brothers and I received at least a university degree or its equivalent.

Many times, her salary was not enough to cover our educational expenses, so she borrowed money to support us. These were not bank loans where repayment could be spread over many years. Often, she borrowed from friends and relatives, sometimes enduring embarrassment and humiliation in the process.

We were all aware of the sacrifices she made for us, and we looked forward to the day when we would finally be able to repay her for all she had done.

Sadly, that opportunity never came.

About ten years before her passing, she was diagnosed with Parkinson's disease. In pain and helplessness, we watched her health gradually deteriorate over the years until she finally passed away on that fateful day.

When I received the phone call, I could not think straight. It felt as though the ground beneath me had suddenly given way. I was still trying to make sense of the loss of my daughter, and now the woman who had given me life was gone too.

In that moment, it felt as though I was losing myself.

****

WHAT REALLY IS GRIEF?

Grief is that emotional pain, that intense sorrow and anguish that we experience when we lose someone or something precious to us. Grief causes us to be deeply distressed and sad because a bond has been broken, either by death, separation, betrayal, or major life changes.

When someone you love is taken away from you especially by the painful hand of death, you grieve because you miss the presence of that person in your life, you miss the value the person adds to you, and the joy you derive from loving and doing life with that person, so the natural response to such loss is grief.

We also grieve when we lose things that are precious to us such as the loss of our health, job, relationships, pet, or a significant life change. For instance, I grieved so

> *We grieve for losing something that once was but no longer is, or for something that should be but is not.*

much at the birth of my daughter because of her medical condition and the challenges ahead of her and me. I grieved for her health, the loss of the freedom to pursue my own dreams and for the disadvantaged position that she seemed to be starting life from. We typically grieve for losing something that once was but no longer is, or for something that should be but is not.

Grief is a deeply personal experience that impacts every aspect of our lives. In addition to the emotional anguish, it also comes with a lot of physical anguish such as aches and pains, exhaustion, loss of appetite, inability to sleep or sleeping too much. It can also exhaust us mentally, as the thoughts of the loss and fear of the unknown preoccupy our minds, leading to confusion, forgetfulness and difficulty in concentration. We will discuss these effects of grief in more details in later chapters.

> *Grieving is therapeutic. It helps us to heal*

However, it is important to note that grieving is therapeutic, and it helps us to heal.

TYPES OF GRIEF

Grief being a complex emotional response to loss, can manifest in different ways depending on the person, the type of loss, and their coping mechanisms. Psychologists and grief experts often categorize grief into several types to help understand and address it more effectively. There are several classifications, but I will explain the most common types here.

Normal (or Uncomplicated) Grief

This is the most common type of grief. It is the natural and expected response to loss that includes emotional, cognitive, physical, and behavioural reactions. With this type of grief, the person still experiences all the common characteristics of grief such as the sadness, anger, guilt, longing for the deceased person and all the emotional pain that accompanies grief, but they gradually decrease over time. The bereaved person can slowly adapt and adjust to life beyond the loss.

"Normal" does not mean "easy." It means that being on this adaptive trajectory, the person does not get stuck in grief. The physical, emotional, and cognitive reactions may be present, but they don't disable the grieving person.

Complicated (Or Prolonged) Grief

This is when grief remains intensely disruptive for a long period (usually more than 12 months) and prevents the person from normal functioning. Complicated grief is often linked to traumatic or sudden losses, lack of support, or previous mental health challenges.

Within Complicated Grief are also other types of grief such as:

- Chronic grief where the grief that never seems to lessen
- Delayed grief where grief is suppressed initially, then resurfaces much later
- Exaggerated grief where grief leads to harmful behaviours (e.g., substance abuse, suicidal thoughts)
- Masked grief where grief symptoms are present, but the person doesn't realise it's related to grief

Anticipatory Grief

This is the grief that is experienced before the actual loss occurs. The expectation that a loss will happen in the future leads to anticipatory grief. It is often common when someone is diagnosed with a terminal illness or in progressive cognitive decline where the person's thinking abilities, memory, and other mental functions are gradually worsening over time.

Anticipatory grief comes with sadness, anxiety, guilt, and emotional preparation for the upcoming loss. However, it helps people to begin processing emotions early, which can ease the transition after the loss occurs.

My friend, Marian Favors who lost her father on the 25th of December 2021 (yes on Christmas day) shared with me how she experienced anticipatory grief even before the actual death of her dad. She said her dad who was ninety years old when he passed, was suffering dementia. Three years before his death, he was unable to speak or recognise his family members. They had to take complete care of him, including getting him up and taking him to the bathroom. She said, seeing her dad in this condition caused her a lot of grief and when he eventually died, she realised that she had processed his death—his emotional death before he died physically.

In her own words, she said, "I feel like I lost my dad three years before I physically lost him, there was an emotional detachment when the dementia set in. I grieved for my father before he died." And she said because she had processed his death emotionally before his physical death, when he eventually died, it just wasn't as impactful as it would have been had he not suffered that illness.

Disenfranchised Grief

This is grief that is not recognised or validated by society. The mourner is not taken seriously, or they are made to feel that they don't have permission to grieve and as a result, they receive no support. Examples of disenfranchised grief are the loss of an ex-partner or affair partner, miscarriage or infertility, loss of a pet, death of loved one who was a criminal, and non-death losses such as divorce and job loss. This type of grief often leads to isolation and suppressed grief responses.

Traumatic Grief

This is the grief that occurs when a loss is so sudden, violent, or horrifying that it overwhelms a person's ability to cope. It combines elements of grief (mourning the loss) and trauma (reacting to a deeply distressing or shocking event). With traumatic grief, the person isn't just grieving, they are also experiencing post-traumatic stress responses tied to the way the death happened.

Examples of cases that result in traumatic grief are deaths through fatal accidents, suicide, homicide, genocide, war or terrorism. The mourner would usually experience post-traumatic stress disorder (PTSD) symptoms like flashbacks, avoidance, and hypervigilance.

Collective or Communal Grief

This is the grief experienced by a community or society after a widespread tragedy. Examples of collective grief is when a community experiences natural disasters, school shootings, terrorist attacks, pandemic losses, genocides or the death of a public figure. The grief is collective because it brings the entire community together to observe rituals, memorials, and shared mourning experiences.

****

CAN YOU EXPERIENCE MULTIPLY TYPES OF GRIEF SIMULTANEOUSLY?

Yes, it is quite common for people to experience multiple types of grief simultaneously or for different forms to overlap or evolve over time. Grief is not linear, and people often move through (or circle back to) different emotional and cognitive responses as they process a loss. I will use the story of my friend, Annick Gakombe, an inspirational speaker and Trauma-informed coach to illustrate this.

Annick's encounter with grief began in 1994 during the genocide against the Tutsi ethnicity group in Rwanda. Before this experience, nothing or no one could have prepared her for what grief truly meant. Up to this time, the only person she had ever known to die was her grandmother on her mother's side. She had been very young at the time, and the connection had not been strong enough for her to fully grasp the meaning of death.

When grief finally came into her life, it arrived abruptly and violently. Annick was the ninth child in her family of twelve that included ten children, her mum and dad. It was a loving Christian family, her dad being a Pastor until everything changed suddenly on this fateful day, the 7th of April 1994 when the genocide struck Rwanda. Annick was only twelve years old when she got separated from her family the very day the genocide started, and she found herself running for her life in the bushes. It was so bad that everyone around her were being hunted and killed like animals. Death became a daily reality, and survival at that time was her only focus as she ran for her life, determined to live.

After one hundred long days in the bushes, sleeping under the rain, sucking water from leaves and eating raw farm produce such as cassava to survive, the genocide eventually ended, and she was looking forward to being reconciled to her family.

The first person that met her was her big brother who had just come into the country because he had been away during the genocide.

He took her to their uncle who broke the news that 'everybody' was gone!

"Gone to where?" Annick wondered. She could not process what she was hearing, her parents and eight siblings had been killed!

The news came like a series of blows revealing that her father, her mother, her siblings—one name after another, were gone, and by the time it got to the sixth, she could feel nothing at all. She was completely numb.

Her uncle, who delivered the news, also told her that his own wife and children, eight in total, had also been killed, leaving him as the only survivor.

Later, Annick met a cousin whose father, mother, and six siblings had also been murdered.

When she saw him, his body bore deep machete wounds, and he carried visible scars of the violence they had all endured. This further increased her shock as she did not know how to think or feel. The loss was not of one person but of an entire world, one that included her family, her safety, and her childhood.

Although she saw many others being killed before her eyes while she ran through the bushes, she never imagined that her own family were also victims. However, she was thankful that she did not witness the death of her family, knowing that there was a difference between seeing strangers die and seeing one's own blood being slaughtered.

For years afterward, Annick moved through life as if in a daze. The whole country was grieving, and at the same time, everyone was trying to return to normal life as if nothing had happened. Families who had fled were coming back. Children were sent back to school. There was a quiet, collective attempt to rebuild amid ruins.

It was not until Annick was around sixteen years old that things began to shift. Her older brother, the only surviving sibling left Rwanda to study in Canada, and with his departure, loneliness crept in. Annick realised for the first time that she missed her parents and her siblings deeply. She began to cry, something she hadn't done in these nearly four years! She had been too busy surviving, moving from one family to another, adapting to new homes and cultures, going to school, simply trying to exist. Her grief was now beginning to surface.

In those years, Rwanda had no emotional support systems. The country was overwhelmed, and there were few, if any, professionals who understood trauma or grief counselling or therapy. Annick was a teenager at this time, and she was in boarding school, surrounded by children from different backgrounds, some of whom were also genocide survivors. Annick noticed that those of them that lived through the genocide had something in common: the sadness, the lack of concentration in classes, the same sudden tears that seemed to come "for no reason" (the reason was there, but neither they nor the people around them understood what was happening). They shared flashbacks, nightmares, and the haunting cries of babies and the images of bodies they had run over during the genocide.

Annick often experienced sleepless nights, reliving the events as though they were happening again. At times, she would be taken to the hospital, sedated until she could rest. When she awoke a day or two later, she would realise she was not back in the genocide, it was her trauma resurfacing. She lived this way for many years, through much of her high school life.

As an orphan, Annick moved from one household to another. In some homes, she was treated with kindness; in others, she was overlooked, mistreated or seen as less than the biological children of the family.

In one of those families she stayed with, she was not even allowed to grieve because they belonged to a different ethnic group; one that had not been targeted during the genocide. Dependent on them for survival, Annick had to suppress her emotions and hide her pain.

UNDERSTANDING THE TYPES OF GRIEF THROUGH ANNICK'S STORY

Annick's grief experience is a very touching and rare one. Her grief experience cuts across many of the different types. It started with Anticipatory Grief, the fear before the loss. Running for her life during the genocide as violence spread through her community, though she didn't yet know who had survived or who had been killed, she lived with the constant dread of loss.

Her grief was traumatic because of the horrifying nature of the deaths, and this was the cause of flashbacks, nightmares, and sleepless nights that she experienced. It was also complicated because of its' prolonged nature, especially because it was delayed. It wasn't until four years later that she began to cry for the first time. When her brother, her last surviving link to family left for Canada, loneliness opened a wound she had buried.

She experienced disenfranchised grief when her grief was not validated and welcomed by the non-Tutsi families she lived with. These families did not understand her pain because they had not been targeted, and depending on them for shelter, she learned to hide her feelings, afraid that expressing sorrow might threaten her safety or belonging.

It was also a collective grief for Rwanda as a nation and particularly the Tutsi ethnic group. After the genocide, grief was everywhere you turn, from the ruins of homes to the empty seats at school, and in the faces of survivors. Till date, over thirty years later, a yearly memorial, where the community come together, is still held in remembrance and honour of their people that died in the genocide.

Recognising the type of grief you may be experiencing will help you to seek the necessary and appropriate support and hence navigate it better.

Chapter 2

WHY IS GRIEF SO AWFUL?

Emma lost her father when she was just thirteen, and that was the first time she truly understood grief. Growing up, she had often heard about relatives passing away, but those losses never fully registered. She only recognised them as sad events without grasping the weight of their implications. Losing her father changed that; it was the first time she truly felt the depth of loss. However, she was able to process her grief by turning to writing for comfort. She poured her emotions into poems and reflections about him and the impact of his death on her family.

Years later, Emma experienced grief again when one of her best friends passed away on the 1st of January 2020. Unlike before, she wasn't able to process that loss. She couldn't write like she did when her dad passed, the words didn't come, and the pain lingered within her.

However, the loss that affected her most deeply was that of her mother in 2022. Emma's mother had undergone surgery for brain aneurysm in 2020, and at the time, Emma had been terrified of losing her. Yet, through faith and prayers, her mother survived the surgery and its complications. By 2021, life was gradually returning to normal. Then, in 2022, her mother began to experience severe headaches, and doctors discovered that the brain aneurysm had reoccurred and that she required another surgery. The fear Emma had felt before returned, but this time her faith was stronger because she reminded herself that God had done it once and He would do it again.

However, the symptoms were more serious this time. Emma's mother, who was usually composed and strong, began to show fear, a rare sight that deeply unsettled Emma. When her mother slipped into a coma, the fear became real. Emma, who was still in school at the time, took a break to stay by her mother's side throughout the ordeal. While her siblings were busy with work and other responsibilities, she became the main point of contact with the doctors and spent every day at the hospital, clinging to hope but haunted by the fear of what might happen.

One day, after rushing home briefly, Emma received a call from the hospital asking her to return immediately, they had been trying to reach her. As she made her way there, she was filled with dread, praying silently that her mother would still be alive. When she arrived, she didn't need the doctors to say anything; their faces told her everything. As they spoke with her sister, Emma asked to see her mother. In that quiet room, facing the stillness of her mother's body, she spoke to her, prayed, and hoped for a miracle, but nothing happened. It was then that she realised the truth that there was nothing more to be done. Her mum was gone!

In shock, Emma left the hospital, unsure where she was going or what she was doing. There wasn't time to process her grief in that moment—there were calls to make, people to notify, and arrangements to handle. When she finally returned home, mourners were already gathering. For days, she was surrounded by people, constantly attending to visitors and responsibilities. Only after the burial did the reality begin to sink in. Even then, she felt numb, unable to fully believe that her mother was truly gone.

****

Asking why grief is so awful is a human question that almost everyone who has experienced grief would have asked at some point. Grief feels so unpleasant because it hits us on every level - emotional, physical, mental, spiritual and even financial.

Here are some reasons grief hurts so much:

Love and loss are two sides of the same coin

Grief hurts so intensely because it comes from love. The deeper and more meaningful a relationship is, the more that person becomes woven into your identity and your daily life. When they're gone, it's not just them you're missing, it's the version of you that existed in relation to them. That's why it feels as though a part of you is gone, too.

When you have a child who is severely disabled and has depended completely on you from birth, the bond you share becomes incredibly strong. In Grace's case, because she couldn't speak, walk, or do anything for herself, I became her voice, her hands, and her legs. As her sisters grew older, they also took on those roles, caring for her and sharing that connection. So, you can imagine the emptiness, waking up and realising that Grace was no longer there to care for. There was a void, a silence that felt unbearable, and that vacuum deepened when all her specialist equipment was removed from her room and the house just a few days after her passing. It was as if her absence became even louder. It truly felt like a part of me was gone. The deeper the bond, the deeper the ache when that bond is broken. Grief, then, is the mind and heart struggling to adjust to a world that suddenly looks and feels different without the person you loved.

Your brain does not understand what has happened at first

The people we love become part of our daily routines and our brain forms habits around them. It knows their voice, their smell, the sound of their footsteps, etc., and when they're gone, the brain keeps expecting them to show up, to call, to walk into the room. That dissonance, expecting them but knowing they won't, is incredibly painful. That is why people often say they "forget" for a moment and think of calling the person who is gone. This is not denial, it is biology.

Angela, who lost her husband to cancer in 2019 tells of how she would often "forget" in those early days that he was dead. She said she was so used to texting and talking to him because they had been very good friends. One day at work, something happened, and Angela grabbed her phone, and started to text him. It was in the middle of texting that she realised, "Oh my gosh, who are you texting? You're not texting anyone." And that, in her own words, "hits you hard and makes you sad."

It takes the brain time to rewire itself to the reality that this person is no longer here physically, and that adjustment period is emotionally brutal.

Grief messes with your sense of control

Loss reminds us that certain things in life are utterly beyond our control, and that realization can be terrifying. We can plan, pray, and prepare, but some things are beyond your power to fix or prevent. This lack of control can make one feel angry, helpless, or even guilty, like you should have done something differently, even if logically you know you couldn't have. This realization can shake your foundation, make you feel unsafe, small, or angry.

Grief exerts a profound physical toll on the body

Studies show that grief activates the same parts of the brain that process physical pain. When experiencing grief, the body's nervous system goes into stress mode. Cortisol, the stress hormone that regulates blood sugar, metabolism, blood pressure, and inflammation rises sharply. Sleep and appetite are disrupted, and the immune system weakens. You might feel exhausted all the time, get sick more easily, or carry a heaviness in your chest that feels impossible to shake.

Every loss I have experienced has left me emotionally drained and physically weak, but the death of my daughter took the deepest toll. Her passing was so sudden that I went into complete shock and disbelief. My blood pressure spiked almost immediately, and when my doctor examined me, she said, "I would be surprised if your BP did not rise."

So, when people say, "grief hurts," they mean it literally. The ache in your heart, the tension in your muscles, the racing heartbeat, the elevated blood pressure, the nausea or dizziness are real, physical manifestations of grief.

Grief shakes your core

Grief doesn't just hurt the heart; it shakes the soul.

When you lose someone you love deeply, it can unsettle the very core of your being. You begin to question things you once felt sure about: *Why did this happen? Where was God? Why them? Why now?*

In moments like these, grief feels like an earthquake that cracks the foundation of your beliefs. Everything that once made sense suddenly doesn't. You might find yourself doubting God, questioning fairness, or feeling disconnected from the person you used to be.

When my daughter, Grace, was born with severe disabilities, I held onto my faith and believed for a miracle that one day she would speak, walk, and grow the limbs she was missing. But when that did not happen before she passed, I was left with many questions. My faith was shaken, and that feeling was awful.

Many people describe this part of grief as a *spiritual fog*. The prayers that once came easily now feel heavy. The songs of hope sound distant. Even Scripture can feel hollow for a while.

Grief touches the wallet, too

Grief can also have a significant impact on our finances, often in ways we do not anticipate. When someone experiences a major loss, especially of a close family member or someone they cared for deeply, the emotional, physical, and practical consequences often ripple into financial life as well.

One of the most immediate effects comes from the costs surrounding death itself — funeral expenses, medical bills, travel arrangements, and legal paperwork. Even when some of these are covered by insurance or community support, unexpected expenses can still pile up quickly, adding another layer of stress to an already painful experience.

Grief also tends to affect income and productivity. Many people find it difficult to return to work right away or to perform at their usual level. Concentration fades, motivation disappears, and energy runs low. For those who are self-employed or work on contracts, this impact can be even more severe, as time off often means no income at all.

In many households, loss brings major lifestyle changes. When the person who passed was the family's main source of income, surviving relatives may be forced to adjust in many ways like moving homes, selling possessions, or learning to live on a single income. Even for those who were not financially dependent, the emotional weight of grief can make managing day-to-day finances challenging.

Beyond the practical changes, grief often takes a physical toll that can create additional costs. Stress-related illnesses, high blood pressure, insomnia, and depression sometimes require ongoing medical care or therapy. The body, already weakened by sorrow, demands more attention, and more financial resources.

In my own experience, the financial impact of grief was unmistakable. Within a three-year period, I lost my father, my mother, and my daughter. At the time, I was working on contract jobs, meaning I was only paid when I worked. Each period of mourning meant time away from work, and therefore, no income. These losses were not only emotionally and physically draining but also financially challenging.

Grief doesn't just live in the heart; it also touches the wallet. It affects how we work, spend, and plan. The financial strain that accompanies loss is one of the hidden burdens of grief, something almost everyone experiences. I illustrated this beautifully in my book, "Through The Storm."

Grief comes in waves

Grief is not linear. It does not follow neat stages that end with "acceptance." It is more like the ocean that is calm one moment and overwhelming the next. You might feel fine for weeks, then suddenly a song, a smell, or an anniversary sends you spiralling back into sadness. That unpredictability can make grief feel endless and exhausting, making it seem like you are not healing, but in truth, it is a normal part of the process. Each wave helps your heart adjust to living with the loss.

Oscar lost his son, Jonny, to heart failure when Jonny was just fourteen years old (I tell the full story in chapter 8). Since then, grief has come to him in waves. Some days feel calm, almost peaceful, while others bring back the pain as if it were new again.

Each time Oscar sees Jonny's classmates, another wave rises. They are now in their second year at the university, and whenever he sees them coming home for the holidays, he can't help but think, *If Jonny were alive, he would have been in year two as well.* Last year, when his mates had their matriculation ceremony, that wave returned—strong and heavy.

Every new milestone his classmates reach reminds Oscar of the future Jonny never got to live. He knows these reminders will continue to come—when they graduate, when they get married, when they start their own families. Each moment brings another quiet ache, another gentle wave of memory and longing.

Yet even in those moments, Oscar finds a way to give thanks. When the sadness hits, he often says, God, I thank You because I still have my other two children. How about those who have none? Those words comfort him and help him stay grounded. They don't erase the pain, but they soften it. It's how Oscar has learned to ride the waves of grief, by holding on to gratitude, even as he holds on to the memory of his son.

DEALING WITH THE AWFULNESS OF GRIEF

With all these difficult truths we have discussed about grief,

I am sure you are wondering how to get rid of the pain and heaviness that come with it. But if we are being honest, you do not really get rid of the awfulness of grief, you learn, slowly and gently, how to live with it.

Over time, the weight becomes a little lighter and more bearable. The ache doesn't completely vanish, but it softens as you learn to carry it differently.

I dedicate a whole chapter to coping with grief, but for now, let's briefly look at a few ways to begin navigating its awfulness.

Accept that grief is not something to "get over"

The awfulness of grief often feels worse when we think it is something we are supposed to fix. But grief isn't a problem to solve, it's a process to live through. The pain lessens with time, but it doesn't vanish. Once you stop fighting it and allow yourself to feel it, the waves begin to soften.

Give yourself permission to feel everything

Grief is messy. A whole lot of emotions can show up at the same time—sadness, anger, guilt, relief, confusion, or even moments of laughter. Every emotion has a place, so allow yourself to feel the full range. You don't have to be strong all the time. Some days you will cry, other days you will smile at a memory and feel a little peace; and both are okay. Grief is made up of both sadness and gratitude, and the two can coexist in the same heart.

Talk about your loved one

Silence makes grief heavier. Say their name, share their stories, and let others know who they were. Keeping their memory alive helps you integrate their absence into your present life. It turns pain into remembrance, and remembrance into love that still lives on.

Find an outlet for expression

Absorbing pain without letting it out is very unhealthy, and that is why it is crucial to find safe ways to release it. You can do this by expressing your emotion in various ways. For some, it is writing, for others, it might be painting, praying, singing or listening to music. Expression gives your grief a voice and allows the pain to move through you instead of getting stuck inside.

Expression gives your grief a voice and allows the pain to move through you instead of getting stuck inside.

Stay connected

It may feel easier to pull away and isolate yourself, but you must be intentional about staying connected even when it is uncomfortable. Grief isolates, but connection heals. You don't always have to talk about your loss but being around people who make you feel safe and seen can remind you that you are still part of life. Let others love you through the silence.

Take care of your body

We have already established that grief is physical. It drains your strength and affects your sleep, appetite, and energy. So, rest when you can, eat something nourishing, take short walks, and give yourself grace on the days you feel too tired to do anything. The body carries grief too, and tending to it helps the mind begin to recover.

Lean on your faith or whatever gives you meaning

As disorienting as it may be when grief shakes your faith, try not to run from it. Let it become a sacred space for honesty. God is not offended by our questions, our anger, or our confusion. He meets us in them. So, sit with it and speak to God honestly, even if all you can say is, "I don't understand" or "Lord, help me." The same God who held you in joy can hold you in your doubt.

Expressing gratitude can also steady you in the midst of loss. It won't take away the ache, but it will bring some comfort and hope. When the waves hit, try to whisper, "Thank You, Lord, for the time I had, for the love I shared, and for the strength to keep going." Those small prayers build quiet courage.

Allow time

Remember that grief comes in waves, and that's normal. Some days will feel calm and others will feel unbearable. When the hard days come, be gentle on yourself and see them as part of the process and reminders of the deep love that runs in you for the person you lost. Healing doesn't mean forgetting, it means remembering with less pain and more love. Over time, the memories that once hurt will begin to bring warmth again. You will never stop missing them, but you will find ways to carry them with you, gently, as you continue to live.

Chapter 3

HOW DO I PROCESS GRIEF?

To process grief means to allow yourself to gradually experience, accept and integrate the reality of a loss emotionally, mentally, and even physically so that the pain of that loss can begin to coexist with your life, rather than control it.

Processing grief means:

Facing reality

When loss initially happens, it can feel unreal. Our minds protect us with denial or numbness where we keep telling ourselves, "This can't be true." Processing begins when we slowly start to accept that the loss really happened and we stop running from the truth of it. It is that moment when your heart starts to catch up with what your mind already knows.

Feeling, not fighting your emotions

Along with sadness, grief comes with many other emotions such as anger, confusion, guilt, fear, emptiness, and

Processing grief is not "getting over it", it is getting through it.

sometimes even relief. To process grief is to let those emotions move through you instead of pushing them away. When you allow yourself to feel, cry, talk, or sit quietly with pain, you are actually helping your body and mind heal. Processing grief is not "getting over it", it is getting through it.

Making sense of your loss

After a loss, our minds are naturally asking questions such as, "Why did this happen? What does this mean for me now?" This is a search for meaning because processing grief includes meaning-making. This helps us to find a way to live in a world that has changed, and to carry the memory of what was lost in a way that still lets you move forward.

Adjusting to a new reality

Grief changes everything including your routines, roles, identity, and even how you see the world. Processing grief involves slowly adapting to life as it is now. This may mean learning to do things alone, rediscovering joy, or finding new sources of comfort and connection.

Carrying the loss with less pain

When you choose to face reality, not fight your emotions, and gradually accept your loss, the sharp edges of grief begin to soften with time. The loss remains part of you, but it stops breaking you. This is when you can remember the experience without being overwhelmed.

STAGES AND THEORIES OF GRIEF

Many experts have done extensive work on grief. As grief can sometimes feel chaotic and impossible to explain, this work in the form of stages and theories helps offer language, validation, and better understanding of grief. They help you understand that grief is normal,

Grief is normal, human, and survivable.

human, and survivable. I will be discussing three of such theories here.

KÜBLER-ROSS MODEL

In her best-selling book, "On Death and Dying" published in 1969, Elisabeth Kübler-Ross, a Swiss-American psychiatrist, discussed her theory of the five stages that people go through when they experience grief. These five stages are **Denial, Anger, Bargaining, Depression and Acceptance** known as Kübler-Ross model for grief. According to Elisabeth's son, Ken Ross, "The five stages are meant to be a loose framework; they're not some sort of recipe or a ladder for conquering grief. If people wanted to use different theories or different models, she didn't care. She just wanted to begin the conversation."[2]

Over time, the Kübler-Ross model was modified to include two additional stages that are prevalent when people experience grief, and these are shock and guilt. This makes the modified Kübler-Ross seven stages of grief to be **Shock**, Denial, Anger, Bargaining, **Guilt**, Depression, and Acceptance. Let me briefly describe each of the stages here.

Shock is the first emotion most people experience when they hear devastating news. It is when you freeze or experience a numbness, and not being able to process the incident. Some people might scream, collapse, or just stare when they experience a shock.

Denial is the emotion that most people experience after shock. It is the struggle to come to terms with reality. Sometimes, due to the suddenness of the loss, it is difficult to believe that it is true, so it becomes easier to deny the reality and say, "No, this can't be true! How can this person die just like that?"

In processing grief, denial is the mind's way of protecting you from the full impact of loss. It creates emotional distance so that you can take in the truth gradually. While in denial, you are still able to function in daily life immediately after loss.

Anger sets in when you realise that your denial doesn't seem to change the situation. It dawns on you that your loved one is gone and you are not going to see them again in this world. You realise that this wasn't a dream after all, and in your attempt to fight against the overwhelming pain accompanying the grief, you get angry. Anger could also be expressed as a feeling of disappointment, sometimes towards God, people, or inanimate objects.

Anger brings energy back after the numbness, and when expressed safely, it can prevent emotions from turning inward which can lead to depression.

Bargaining is your attempts to make deals that could change the situation. Sometimes you find yourself trying to make a deal with God by saying, "If you can change this situation, I will do this or I will do that or I will turn my life around."

Depression is a state of profound sadness that sets in when you fully grasp what you have lost. It is a state where the grieving person is in a very low mood and loses interest and enjoyment in things[6]. It is the moment when denial breaks and bargaining has not changed the situation. This is a natural state of grief and not clinical depression.

In processing grief, you need to allow yourself to feel it rather than avoiding it as this helps to release long-held pain. However, if hopelessness lasts too long or becomes unbearable, it may turn into clinical depression and that is when professional help becomes vital. So watch out for prolonged despair and seek help as quickly as possible

Guilt is that emotional state where you may begin to blame and beat yourself down. You feel that if you took certain actions, the loss could have been prevented and so you are filled with regret. You wish you could turn the hand of the clock and do things differently.

Acceptance is when you come to terms with the situation, realising that there is nothing you can do to change it. Your loved one is gone, and you cannot bring them back to life so you accept your reality, and by accepting it, you find a way to move forward.

From my personal experience and in interacting with others, I agree with Ken Ross that this model is a loose framework to understand our emotional reactions to grief and not some sort of recipe or a ladder for conquering grief.

In as much as most people will experience the emotions mentioned in this model, they do not necessarily go through them linearly. That is to say that one does not have to go from shock to denial to anger to bargaining to guilt to depression and finally acceptance. Some people may not experience some of the emotions at all, and some may bounce back and forth between these emotions. That is to say that someone who seemed to have accepted the situation today, may find themselves bouncing back to anger or even depression the following day. So, rather than view this model as the *stages* of grief, I prefer to look at it as the various *states* of emotions that people can find themselves when grieving.

The model does not tell you how to grieve but it helps you understand what's happening as you do. It turns an overwhelming storm of emotions into something you can observe, name, and gently move through. Even though grief remains uniquely personal, having a map, even if it is a rough one, helps you walk through the darkness with a little more light.

> *Grief remains uniquely personal, but having a map, even if it is a rough one, helps you walk through the darkness with a little more light*

WORDEN'S TASKS OF MOURNING

J. William Worden, a prominent grief theorist, introduced the "Four Tasks of Mourning" model in his book Grief Counselling and Grief Therapy, first published in 1983, with the latest edition being the 5th edition published in 2018. He said that undertaking these tasks of mourning by anyone grieving can help them to navigate grief and adapt to life after a loss.

Unlike the more rigid idea of "stages," he emphasised that these are just tasks that people can work through to move through grief back and forth as they process their loss, and it doesn't necessarily have to be followed in a linear order. Different people move at different paces and there's no set timeline for grief. He differentiated between the terms 'grief' and 'mourning', saying that grief is the personal experience of loss, while mourning is the process that occurs after the loss. However, these terms are often used interchangeably by most theorists, and I will be doing the same in this book.

These tasks acknowledge that grief is both emotional and active: it's something we do, not just something we feel. I will briefly explain the four tasks below.

Task 1: To Accept the Reality of the Loss

It's often very difficult to accept the reality that someone we love or know is dead even when we saw the death coming. And this is most difficult when the death happens to be sudden and unexpected.

According to Worden, the first task of grieving is to come to terms with the reality that the person is dead, gone and will not return. He said that part of the acceptance of this reality is coming to believe that reunion is impossible, at least in this life.

To accept this reality as someone who is grieving, you may need to say it aloud repeatedly to yourself, "They are gone, and they're not coming back!"

Accepting the loss intellectually is a lot easier than accepting it emotionally, and most people who have experienced loss can attest to this fact.

Emma, a young lady who lost her mom in 2022 talks about the difficulty of accepting her death even more than three years down the line. She told me a story about her brother who had just had a baby, and she went to visit them in the hospital. She said during the visit, she felt unsettled, trying to peep outside the hospital building, and guess who she was looking out for? Her mom!

She said she kept thinking to herself, "Mummy will soon arrive, and my brother would tell me to go and bring her upstairs."

She said it felt only natural for her mom to be at the bedside of her grandchild. She said she was in this expectant mode until the doctor came around and said he wanted to talk to the entire family because there were a few complications with the baby after birth.

It was when the doctor asked her brother, "Is this everybody we need to speak to? Is there anyone else?"

And her brother answered, "Yes, this is everybody, there is no other person," that it hit her, "Oh, mom is not coming."

She said, even though her mom has been dead for a couple of years, she still expected her to be there, and there was a feeling of disappointment and sadness when she didn't show up. Even though Emma knew intellectually that her mom was dead, it is taking a while for her emotions to catch up.

Emma's story reminds us that we need to be patient with ourselves and allow time for our emotions to accept the reality of the loss. Emma may have to keep telling herself repeatedly, "My mom is dead, she's not coming back, I'm not going to see her in this world again," until her emotions accepts that reality and stop expecting her to show up.

During this task of mourning, belief and disbelief tend to alternate as sometimes, it may seem like you have accepted the reality, while at other times, you may be swayed away by the illusion of seeing and reuniting with the dead person again. To handle this task, you need to ensure that you are continually facing and addressing your loss, and not denying, minimising, or avoiding it.

Traditional rituals such as attending the funeral of the deceased person often move you toward acceptance. Those not present during this event may need other ways of validating the reality of the loss so that they can accept it. Other activities like holding a memorial service for the deceased, getting rid of their belongings or packing them up, reading their will or handling their other affairs can also help acceptance to set in.

Task 2: To Process the Pain of Grief

C. Murray Parkes, a British psychiatrist and researcher who is internationally recognised for his pioneering work on grief, bereavement, and palliative care, said in his book, *Bereavement: Studies of Grief in Adult Life (1972)*, "If it is necessary for the bereaved person to go through the pain of grief in order to get the grief work done, then anything that continually allows the person to avoid or suppress this pain can be expected to prolong the course of mourning."

The pain of grief is intense, and it is often an uphill task to process this pain. However, to heal from grief, you need to allow yourself to feel this pain, not escape, suppress or ignore it. People sometimes prevent this task by using alcohol or drugs, idealising the deceased, and avoiding reminders of the deceased. While others try to bypass this task through distractions, overworking, or emotional shutdown. I want you to note that the grief that you do not take time to process can show up later in ways that are detrimental to your wellbeing such as through physical symptoms, ailments and unusual behaviours.

> *The pain of grief is intense. However, to heal from grief, you need to allow yourself to feel this pain, not escape, suppress or ignore it.*

Some of the pain that we can allow ourselves to feel during this task include sadness, anger, guilt, fear, relief, or deep yearning. If you are struggling to process the pain of grief, you may want to consider grief counselling, because this is one of the aims of counselling. Worden warns that if this task is avoided or not adequately addressed, complicated or prolonged grief can arise, and therapy may be needed at that stage.

I understand that different cultures, families, or personal experiences can affect how openly people process grief, and I will discuss that in more details later. There's no "right" way to feel.

Task 3: To Adjust to a World Without the Deceased

In tackling this task, Worden talks about three areas of adjustments that need to be addressed after the death of a loved one. These three areas are external adjustments, internal adjustments and spiritual adjustments.

External adjustments

This is the impact of the loss on one's everyday functioning in the world. The death of a loved one can have different impact on different people, depending on the role that this person played in their lives. We are not usually aware of the role people play in our lives until they are no more. And Worden said this realisation often begins to set in around three to four months after they are gone. For a widow, this could involve coming to terms with living alone, taking on new roles such as being the sole provider and defender for the family. These external adjustments can lead to making meaning from the loss.

Internal adjustments

This is the impact of the loss on one's sense of self. There is often identity shifts associated with losses. Suddenly, you realise that you are no longer a wife, your dad's favourite daughter, a best friend, etc. Death affects our self-definition, self-esteem and self-efficacy (the degree to which we feel we have control over what happens to us). We must understand that this adjustment is not only needed in deaths but in all forms of losses. I remember how I needed to make these adjustments after my divorce because as women, oftentimes, we define ourselves through our relationships, I am Mrs..., I am this person's wife, etc. The internal task for someone mourning is to address questions like: Who am I now? What makes me unique outside of my lost relationship or deceased loved one? These internal adjustments may take time, but it is a necessary task to undertake as you process your grief.

Spiritual Adjustments

This is the influence of the loss on one's values, beliefs, and assumptions about the world. Loss, especially through death can challenge one's fundamental beliefs, values and world views, where we find ourselves questioning what we once believed and valued. This is when we begin to ask questions like; Why did this happen? What does this mean for me now? Can someone help me make it make sense?

However, when a death is expected, it does not challenge our beliefs and values but rather validates them. An example of this is when an elderly person dies honourably. When this task is not sufficiently addressed, there will be a failure to adjust to the loss. People in this situation may find themselves promoting their own helplessness by not developing the skills they need to cope.

Task 4: To Find an Enduring Connection with the Deceased While Moving Forward with Life

This task is intended to provide a place that helps the bereaved to lead a fruitful life in the world. Worden interpreted this task as "finding a way to remember the deceased while embarking on the rest of one's journey through life". The task means that you can still carry their memory and yet live a fulfilling life.

This is not about "letting go" in the traditional sense. Instead, it's about finding a new kind of relationship with the person or thing lost. You move from physical presence to emotional presence such as memories, legacies, values, or lessons that continue. You begin to reinvest in various aspects of your life such as relationships, personal development, and your vision. While creating a ritual or legacy that honours the deceased, you make space for things that bring you joy without feeling guilty.

For many people, tackling this task is the most difficult as many get stuck in grief, unable to move forward or fully live after a loss. And this is where grief coaching can complement counselling and help the bereaved move forward.

THE MOURNING PROCESS – MEDIATORS OF MOURNING

According to Worden, the tasks of mourning is just one aspect of the mourning process. The second aspect which is important to know, is the mediators of mourning, which refer to the factors that influence how a person experiences, expresses, and adapts to grief after a loss. These mediators help explain why people grieve differently and why the grieving process varies in duration and intensity.

The seven mediators of mourning introduced by Worden (2010) are:

1. Who the person who died was
2. The nature of the attachment
3. How the person died
4. Historical antecedents:
5. Personality variables
6. Social variables
7. Concurrent stressors

Let me briefly explain each of the mediators:

Mediator 1: Who the person who died was

This refers to the relationship between the bereaved and the deceased. The degree of closeness and dependency significantly influences the intensity of grief. The loss of a spouse, child, parent, or distant relative will be experienced differently. For example, the death of a spouse or child often results in a deeper level of grief than the loss of an elderly parent.

The depth of the emotional connection also plays an important role. For example, two daughters who have lost their father may grieve in very different ways because their relationships with him were shaped by their ages and individual experiences. The 14-year-old's understanding, expectations, and memories of her father differ greatly from those of her 2-year-old sister. These unique experiences and hopes influence the intensity and nature of each child's grief.

Mediator 2: The nature of the attachment

This refers to the bond between the bereaved person and the one who has died. Generally, the stronger the bond, the more intense the experience of grief. When the love is deep, the grief is often felt in equal measure. However, ambivalence or unresolved conflict within the relationship can complicate the grieving process, often resulting in feelings such as guilt.

The nature of the attachment may also influence how the survivor experiences loss. For instance, if the bereaved person's sense of self-worth or identity was closely tied to the deceased, their grief may be more profound. Similarly, dependence on the deceased for practical or emotional support such as managing finances, driving, or preparing meals, can heighten the sense of loss.

Mediator 3: How the person died

Traditionally, deaths are classified under the NASH categories: Natural, Accidental, Suicidal, and Homicidal.

This mediator highlights that sudden or unexpected deaths often lead to more intense or prolonged grief because there is little time for emotional preparation. In contrast, anticipated deaths, such as those following a long illness, may allow for anticipatory grieving, giving loved ones some time to begin processing the loss before it occurs.

Deaths by suicide, homicide, or violent disasters tend to bring additional layers of trauma, stigma, or complicated grief, making it harder for the bereaved to find meaning or closure. Furthermore, experiencing multiple losses within a short period can lead to grief overload, overwhelming the person's coping capacity.

Mediator 4: Historical antecedents

Understanding someone's previous grief experiences, how they have handled it and whether they had any unresolved grief, can provide valuable insight into how their current loss may affect them. This involves exploring their past coping mechanisms and assessing how effective those strategies were.

A history of mental health challenges, such as depression or anxiety, or previous traumatic experiences can also influence how someone grieves in the present. Likewise, repeated or cumulative losses may intensify grief reactions. Individuals who have struggled with past losses or carry unresolved trauma often find the mourning process more challenging.

Mediator 5: Personality variables

This mediator refers to the individual characteristics that influence how a person experiences and manages grief. These include one's coping style (for instance, whether the mourner uses active coping strategies or relies on avoidance coping), attachment style, temperament, personal resilience, age, gender, and cultural or spiritual beliefs that shape how meaning is made from the loss. These variables are discussed in more details in the next chapter.

Overall, individuals with flexible coping skills, secure attachments, and strong internal resources are generally better equipped to adjust to loss and manage the mourning process in a healthy way.

Mediator 6: Social variables

This refers to the amount and quality of social support a mourner receives. Support from family, friends, or the community can play a crucial role in buffering the emotional distress that accompanies grief. Research shows that when bereaved individuals perceive strong social support, it can significantly reduce the negative impact of grief-related stress.

Social variables also include cultural and religious expectations surrounding mourning and the ways in which grief may be expressed. For instance, some cultures encourage open emotional expression, while others promote restraint and quiet endurance.

In many cases, mourners receive an outpouring of support leading up to and during the funeral. However, once the ceremony is over, this support often diminishes as the people giving the support return to their own affairs, sometimes leaving the bereaved feeling abandoned or isolated. This raises an important question: do people withdraw because they believe the grief ends with the funeral, or because they expect the mourner to "move on"?

A lack of ongoing social support or prolonged isolation can hinder emotional healing and may complicate the grieving process, making it harder for individuals to adjust to their loss.

Mediator 7: Concurrent stressors

This refers to other stressful life events that occur around the time of the loss or crisis that arise following the death such as job loss, relocation, financial hardship, health challenges, or other major life transitions.

When multiple stressors occur simultaneously, they can overload a person's coping capacity, making it harder to process grief and potentially delaying or complicating the mourning process.

DUAL PROCESS MODEL

Another grieving model is the Dual Process Model of Grieving, developed by psychologists Margaret Stroebe and Henk Schut in 1999. This is a widely respected framework that describes how people cope with grief following a loss. It emphasizes that grieving is not a linear process but involves an ongoing oscillation between different kinds of coping.

The model identifies two types of coping processes:

1. Loss-Oriented Coping

This process involves directly engaging with the emotions and pain of the loss. It is the emotional and reflective aspect of grieving, where the mourner confronts the reality of the death and begins to process their feelings.

Through activities and thoughts connected to the deceased such as yearning for them, crying or expressing sadness or anger, talking about them, visiting their grave, looking at photos, or reflecting on the circumstances of their death, the mourner gradually works through their emotional pain.

This form of coping closely aligns with Tasks 1, 2, and 4 of Worden's Tasks of Mourning, which emphasize accepting the reality of the loss, processing the pain of grief, and finding an enduring connection with the deceased while moving forward with life.

2. Restoration-Oriented Coping

This process involves adjusting to life without the deceased and focusing on developing new roles, identities, and routines. It represents the more practical and forward-looking aspect of coping.

During this stage, the bereaved person learns new skills and begin to take on new responsibilities such as managing finances or household tasks once handled by the deceased, while also re-engaging with life through work, or hobbies and forming new relationships. This aspect of coping closely corresponds to Task 3 of Worden's Tasks of Mourning, which emphasizes adjusting to a world without the deceased.

The Key Idea of this Dual Process model is the oscillation. Instead of focusing solely on the grief all the time or being on the other extreme end of pushing it away completely, the model proposes the idea that healthy grieving involves moving back and forth between these two modes:

- Grieving and engaging with the pain of the loss
- Taking breaks from grief to restore and function in daily life

This oscillation allows people to process their loss in manageable doses. It normalizes the idea that people don't grieve in a fixed pattern. It explains why it's okay (and healthy) to have days where you don't think about your loss constantly. Applying this model helps avoid burnout from continuous emotional distress by allowing space for recovery and adaptation.

THE WAVE THEORY OF GRIEF

The Wave Theory of Grief is based on the above Dual Process Model (Stroebe & Schut, 1999). The idea behind this theory is that grief comes in waves. When someone experiences a major loss, the pain doesn't move neatly through the five stages of denial, anger, bargaining, depression, and acceptance, described by Elisabeth Kübler-Ross. Instead, grief tends to rise and fall like waves. Sometimes the waves are small and manageable; other times, they crash hard and knock you down unexpectedly.

At first, the waves are constant and crushing. Grief hits hard, often, and can be triggered by anything such as a smell, a song, a familiar place, or a memory. Over time, the waves usually become less frequent and less intense, though they rarely disappear completely. You might go days or weeks feeling okay, and then suddenly, an anniversary or a memory brings another wave. That does not mean you have gone backward; it's simply how grief flows.

The Wave Theory helps people understand that:

- It is normal to have both good days and bad days.
- Feeling okay does not mean you have "forgotten" your loved one.

- Having a difficult day, months or even years later does not mean you are broken or stuck.

This perspective removes the pressure to "get over it" and instead reframes grief as something you learn to live with, something you gradually learn to ride, like learning to stay afloat as the tide changes. And over time, you do become better at navigating the waves.

Chapter 4

HOW ARE YOU COPING?

In November 2024, Mr. Fortune Osemudia experienced one of the most painful moments of his life, the passing of his father at the age of 77. He lost his mother in 1985, nearly forty years before this fateful day, yet his father had never remarried. Speaking about death, he reflected, it is just 'news' to hear it happen to other people; but when it happens personally, the reality and weight of loss are far deeper than words can express.

There were three children in the family, and as the only son, he shared a particularly close bond with his dad. His father had single-handedly raised them, and their relationship was filled with mutual affection and respect. The loss was unexpected and devastating.

It happened on the evening of 19th November 2024, when Mr. Fortune Osemudia received a sudden phone call from family members who said they did not understand what had happened to his father. He was told that his father had simply laid down to rest and they came to find him dead.

Mr. Osemudia was shocked! "But he spoke with me this morning, and told me for he went for exercise," he recalled.

Just the day before, he had visited his father after he received a phone call from him complaining of a stomach-ache. They had spent time together talking and laughing. So, it was a truly shocking experience when he heard of his death the next day.

What made the loss even more painful was the thought that his father had endured so much hardship after losing his wife four decades earlier. He had remained single, despite his children's encouragement to remarry, and spent much of his life in solitude.

"We wanted him to enjoy life again, to experience comfort and happiness," Mr. Osemudia said. "But that never happened, and that was the most painful part," he lamented. "Now that his children are successful and wanted to reward him with some comfort and material things, he has passed away."

One of the most heartbreaking aspects of the loss was the home Mr. Osemudia had been building as a surprise gift for his father. He had kept the project a secret, hoping to present it when it was completed. After his father's passing, visiting the building site filled him with sorrow, as it now felt like a dream left unfulfilled.

"Each time I get to that building, it just feels like a waste of effort," he shared. "It makes me wonder what exactly we are doing here on earth."

His father was buried in January 2025, but even months later, Mr. Osemudia found the grief difficult to overcome. He initially tried to keep himself busy to distract his mind, yet many everyday moments and memories continually reminded him of his father's absence. He is now embracing some active coping mechanism to cope with his grief.

For Mr. Osemudia, his father's death remains one of the deepest and most personal losses of his life, a reminder of love, sacrifice, and the fragility of life.

****

Although grief is a universal human experience, it remains deeply personal, and there is no single "right" way to cope with it. The way individuals experience, and express grief varies widely, as it is influenced by numerous personal, social, and situational factors. While some people can navigate loss with relative resilience, others may struggle for prolonged periods. Grief often evokes intense and unpredictable emotions that can fluctuate over time. As discussed in the previous chapter on processing grief, acknowledging and confronting these emotions is an essential part of healing. However, many individuals attempt to avoid their feelings rather than face them directly.

From a psychological perspective, humans generally adopt one of two primary approaches when dealing with grief, trauma, or other stressful situations: avoidance or confrontation.

These are known as avoidant and active coping mechanisms, respectively. Both strategies serve as ways to mitigate the negative effects of stress. When faced with stress, the sympathetic nervous system activates the body's stress response, preparing it to handle perceived threats. This physiological reaction often referred to as the "fight or flight" response includes increased heart rate, rapid breathing, elevated blood pressure, the release of glucose into the bloodstream, and heightened alertness. These changes provide the energy and strength needed to either confront the threat ("fight") or escape from it ("flight").

While this response is highly effective in situations of immediate physical danger, and are designed for short-term application, the human body does not distinguish between physical threats and emotional stressors. As a result, emotional distress triggers the same physiological reactions. When this stress response is sustained over long periods, it can lead to chronic stress, contributing to various physical and mental health problems. To cope with these challenges and regulate their stress levels, individuals tend to engage either avoidant or active coping mechanisms.

AVOIDANT COPING MECHANISM

These are strategies that individuals use to distance themselves from painful thoughts, emotions, or situations rather than confronting them directly. This occurs when a person ignores or suppresses the underlying issue causing emotional distress, which in this case is grief, and instead, they take on behaviours that make them to avoid thinking about their loss, feeling the emotions, or facing any issues arising from it.

In the context of grief, avoidance can feel protective in the short term, as it temporarily reduces emotional discomfort and allows individuals to function during periods of intense pain. However, over time, this approach often hinders emotional healing and can prolong psychological distress. Research indicates that avoidant emotional coping is associated with a higher risk of developing post-traumatic stress disorder (PTSD) and complicated grief, as unresolved emotions remain unprocessed.

Here are a few ways that people typically do this.

1. Substance Abuse

Some individuals turn to substances such as alcohol, cigarettes, or drugs to cope with the pain of loss. These substances may temporarily numb emotional pain or distract from distressing thoughts, providing a short-lived sense of relief. However, substance use does not address the underlying issue, it merely postpones the emotional work that grief requires. Once the effects wear off, the painful reality often resurfaces, prompting continued use of the substance. Over time, this pattern can lead to dependency or addiction. Rather than alleviating the problem, substance abuse compounds it, resulting in additional physical, emotional, and financial strain. Individuals who find themselves trapped in this cycle become burdened by new challenges such as health complications, strained relationships, and depleted resources. Ultimately, using substances as an avoidance strategy hinders healing and often worsens one's overall well-being.

2. Busyness

Another common avoidant coping strategy is excessive busyness. Some individuals immerse themselves in work or constant activity to distract from the pain of their loss. By staying perpetually occupied, taking on extra projects, extending work hours, or filling every moment with tasks, they leave little room to think about or feel their grief. While maintaining a routine can provide structure and stability in the early stages of loss, overworking or constant activity as a means of avoidance can lead to burnout and emotional exhaustion. In essence, the individual becomes so busy trying not to feel that they lose touch with their emotional needs.

So, let me ask: Are you hiding your pain behind your work or constant busyness?

Facing grief, instead of outrunning it, is essential for genuine healing.

> *Facing grief, instead of outrunning it, is essential for genuine healing*

3. Distraction and Pleasure-Seeking

Distraction through play or entertainment is another way people avoid confronting their grief. This may involve immersing oneself in physical games, video games, endless scrolling on social media, or constant consumption of movies and online content. Such distractions can provide momentary comfort and mental escape, helping individuals manage overwhelming emotions in the short term. However, when used excessively, these behaviours become a form of avoidance that prevents emotional processing.

Time spent in constant distraction not only delays healing but can also lead to unproductivity and detachment from meaningful relationships or responsibilities. Moderation is key, while short breaks for leisure can be healthy, relying on distraction to suppress grief only postpones the necessary journey toward acceptance and recovery.

4. Denial

Denial, identified by Elisabeth Kübler-Ross as one of the five stages of grief, is a normal and often necessary reaction when a loss first occurs. It serves as a psychological buffer, shielding the individual from immediate emotional pain and postponing the full confrontation with grief. In the short term, denial can be adaptive, allowing the bereaved person time to gradually adjust to their new reality. However, when denial persists and an individual continues to minimize or reject the reality of their loss as a defence against emotional pain, it becomes an avoidant coping mechanism. Prolonged denial prevents emotional processing and may lead to emotional stagnation, leaving the person "stuck" in an unresolved state of mourning.

5. Social Withdrawal

This happens when grieving individuals isolate themselves from friends, family, or social activities in their bid to reduce exposure to emotional triggers such as sympathy, reminders of the deceased, or conversations about the loss. They might avoid gatherings, stop communicating with others, or prefer being alone most of the time. By withdrawing, the person avoids situations that could intensify painful feelings.

In the short-term, it can provide temporary relief and space for reflection. However, prolonged withdrawal can deepen feelings of loneliness, depression, and detachment.

It also deprives the person of the social support networks that are essential for emotional recovery.

6. **Blame** (self and others)

Blame can manifest in two forms: self-blame, directed inward like "It's my fault they died", and other-blame, directed outward like "If the doctors had acted faster, they would still be here". Both serve as a form of avoidance because it shifts the focus from the raw emotional pain of loss to a more controllable or intellectualized narrative. Instead of confronting the grief pain directly, the grieving person channels their emotions into guilt, anger, or resentment. Yet over time, self-blame can lead to deep feelings of guilt and shame, while blaming others can breed bitterness and hinder forgiveness, both of which obstruct the natural healing process.

ACTIVE COPING MECHANISM

As the name implies, this approach involves taking intentional steps to face the issue of concern, which in this case is grief. It is a healthier and the most effective way to cope with the pain and stress that grief brings.

When you are experiencing grief, it doesn't matter how openly or quietly you express your emotions. What truly matters is your commitment to finding active and healthy ways to manage them.

Below are some practical, healthy steps you can take to work through grief:

1. Positive reframing

This is when we look for the good in a seemingly bad situation, try to focus on that 'good' and interpret the situation from the lens that 'good'. In other words, we choose to view or think about the situation from a positive angle. When grief hits us, it can be very challenging to see any good in the situation, especially at the early stages of grief but through quiet reflections and prayers if you are a person of faith, you will begin to see the positives.

When my daughter, Grace, passed in 2019, all I saw and felt at first was pain, waste and unfairness, and I will tell you why.

Losing any loved one is painful but the pain of losing a child is almost unbearable, so I felt this intense pain at her loss. She was a child with special needs for whom I had given up virtually everything to care for. At the time of her death, it felt like I had wasted the fifteen and half years I had poured into raising and caring for her, and that feeling in itself was painful.

I also felt like her death was quite unfair because all that preoccupied my mind was, "Why would God give me a child that I needed to learn new skills, make a lot of life adjustments and sacrifices to be able to properly care for, and just when it seems like I was getting good at it, He takes her away from me?" I felt pain and emptiness, I felt cheated, because I thought I had a deal with God to heal and perfect her health. Afterall, I was serving Him and using my painful experiences to help others (I tell the story behind using my pain for the gain of others in my book, *He Gave Me Comfort*).

I guess you may also be feeling this way after your loss, and it's natural to feel there are no positives in your loss. But as I began to reflect on who I have become as a result of having and raising Grace, the blessings she brought into my life and most importantly how I found my life's purpose through my experience with her, I then realised that there was 'good' in this experience after all.

With positive reframing, you're not undermining the importance of your loss, but you just choose to focus and appreciate the good times you have had with this person, the good memories you created with them, the value they added to you, the lessons you have learned through their lives and your relationship with them, and the positive legacy you want their lives to represent. You will realise that as you begin to reframe your thoughts and the actions you take based on these thoughts, the pain of grief will gradually begin to ease.

2. Humour

"A happy heart is good medicine *and* a joyful mind causes healing, But a broken spirit dries up the bones."[26]

There are not many things that will crush you like grief so finding ways to distract yourself through humour is a wise thing to do. Many believe that you should never crack a joke around a grieving person so that it doesn't feel like you are disregarding their grief but that is far from the truth. If you can say or do something that will make a grieving person laugh, you have given them a dose of good medicine towards their healing.

I remember this family friend that came to visit us a few days after my daughter's passing. The atmosphere in the house was tense with grief, but he started telling some funny jokes that made all of us laugh so much and this made the atmosphere lighter. In fact, days after his visit, some of those jokes he told will play back in my mind and I will smile even amid my grief.

I also remember when the head teacher from Grace's school was giving a tribute at her funeral. Her tribute was about the funny and 'mischievous' things Grace used to do while she was in school. Grace was severely disabled so people would often overlook her and consider her incapable of doing certain things. But as this head teacher made jokes about these things Grace used to do, we found ourselves smiling and laughing at the funeral even with tears in our eyes, as we fondly remembered her. Today, when I go back and look at the photos taken on that day and see the smile on our tear-stained faces, I still smile, and it makes me wonder how one can still laugh even when hurting.

I must however caution that you must be careful about the kind of jokes you tell around someone who is grieving. You must be very sensitive to them. Never tell jokes that seem to mock their feelings or the memory of their loved one. If your joke doesn't land well, then stop immediately and switch to something else. Their reaction to the joke will tell you if it is appropriate or not.

For you who is grieving, you may not have people around you to create the humour you need. So, you can actively find ways to get humour to help you cope with grief. Recollecting funny memories with your loved one, watching a comedy show or going through funny pictures from the past are ways to make yourself smile, and who knows, you may even have a good belly laugh, and this will do you good like a medicine.

Remember that the goal is not to dismiss or disregard the importance of your loss but rather, it's a way to help you hold on to more positive emotions and help you cope with the grief.

3. Faith

As a person of faith, I would like to share how my faith has helped me to actively deal with grief and heal. If faith is not something you connect with and are not open to knowing about it, please feel free to skip this section.

My faith in God and His Word has been my greatest assets when dealing with grief. God invites us in His Word to,

"Come to me, all you who are weary and burdened, and I will give you rest. Take my yoke upon you and learn from me, for I am gentle and humble in heart, and you will find rest for your souls. For my yoke is easy and my burden is light."[29]

A yoke is a wooden frame placed on an animal's neck to help it pull a cart, so the "yoke" referred to in this passage symbolizes the commitment of following Jesus, while the "burden" represents the responsibilities that come with that choice. Although being a follower of Jesus involves certain demands, they cannot be compared to the weight of the burden we carry when we try to handle life's struggles on our own.

Grief is a burden far too heavy to be carried alone, but when we come to God, we can exchange this heavy burden of grief for the light burden of following and obeying His instructions. You have the privilege of bringing every concern before Him in prayer, and as you do, you will find that your relationship with Him becomes your deepest source of comfort and strength during times of loss. The journey to healing from grief becomes a lot easier and faster when we walk with God. I have experienced this personally,

Grief is a burden far too heavy to be carried alone

and you can too. Faith in God helps us find meaning in our grief, connect with a higher purpose, and draw comfort from the promise of a pain-free eternity.

4. Accepting support

This is an active step that involves reaching out to others and allowing them to be part of your healing process. Often, the people or community around the bereaved person may not know exactly how to support them. This is when it becomes crucial for this person to reach out for help. When a person chooses to lean on friends, family, faith communities, or support groups, they are taking deliberate action to connect rather than withdraw.

I remember when my mum passed just three months after the death of my daughter. I felt so overwhelmed by the news that I couldn't even think straight, talk less of processing the grief. I reached out to a Facebook community that I belonged to, and straight away, the support began to pour in. By the following day, I felt the overwhelm shifting and I could then think.

Grief often brings feelings of isolation and helplessness, but accepting help enables others to provide comfort, understanding, and practical assistance. This shared experience not only lightens the emotional burden but also helps the grieving person feel seen and validated. Emotional support from others can reinforce a sense of belonging and hope, reminding individuals that they are not alone in their pain. By embracing the care and encouragement of others, one cultivates resilience and lays a stronger foundation for recovery.

5. Venting your feelings

Venting your feelings is an important and active way to cope with grief because it allows you to acknowledge, express, and release the emotions associated with loss. Suppressing grief often prolongs emotional pain, while expressing it helps you process it in healthy ways. There are many ways to vent your feelings, depending on your personality, comfort level, and emotional needs.

Below are some effective approaches you may want to consider:

i. Crying

Crying is a natural and healthy emotional release. It allows your body to physically express sorrow, providing relief and reducing emotional tension. Depending on your personality, you may cry quietly or scream as you weep but ensure that you let out those emotions. Many people find that after crying, they feel calmer and more at peace.

ii. Talking to someone you trust

One of the most direct ways to vent your feelings is by talking to someone who listens without judgment such as a close friend, family member, counsellor, therapist, grief coach or faith leader. Verbalizing your emotions helps you make sense of what you're going through and when you are being listened to with understanding and empathy, you feel comforted.

Remember the popular saying that, "A problem shared is a problem halved." Talking about your feelings and fears to a trusted person offloads the heavy burden you are carrying and simply being heard can bring a sense of relief.

Moreover, a grief professional provides a safe and confidential environment to explore your feelings in depth. In talking to them, they can help you understand your emotions, identify coping patterns, and find constructive ways to manage your grief.

6. Joining a support group

Support groups, whether in person or online, provide a safe space to share your grief with others who have experienced similar losses. Find a group whose values and beliefs align with yours. One of my daughters joined a "Grief Share" support when she lost her sister, and she affirmed how helpful that group was to her, especially as she was living abroad at that time and didn't have close family members around her.

Sharing your story and hearing others' experiences can validate your emotions, reduce feelings of isolation, strengthen relationships and foster healing through shared understanding. However, you should also know when it's time to move forward from the group so that you don't get caught up in a cycle of romanticising your grief.

7. Writing or Journaling

This has been one of my greatest outlets for processing and being able to cope with grief, and it is what led to my first book, "He Gave Me Comfort." Writing about your thoughts and feelings is a powerful form of emotional release. Your writing can be letters to the person you lost, documenting a memoir of your journey, or simply describing how you feel day to day.

Journaling allows you to express thoughts and emotions that may be difficult to say aloud and can help you track your healing process and identify patterns of growth.

8. Creative expression

Expressing grief through creative outlets such as painting, drawing, music, dance, poetry, or storytelling can be deeply therapeutic. Creative expression gives emotions a tangible form and allows pain to be transformed into something meaningful or even beautiful.

My daughter, Eyum-Priscilla, for instance, wrote many beautiful poems about her sister after she passed away. She shared one of those poems during the funeral, and it deeply moved and captivated everyone present. Similarly, I began my podcast as a creative avenue to share my story and to provide a platform for others to share theirs.

For Mr. Fortune Osemudia, whose story I shared at the beginning of this chapter, music became a powerful source of healing after the devastation of the sudden death of his father. As a gospel music artist, he saw that difficult season as an opportunity to reconnect with some of his earlier songs that he had not worked on for a long time. He devoted more time and attention to his music because it brought him relief and comfort. During that period, he found himself singing more frequently, not as a form of work, but as a way to soothe his grief. Music became a healing outlet for him, offering solace and renewed strength when he needed it most.

One remarkable truth about expressing grief through creative outlets is that it is a win–win experience. While the act of creation is deeply therapeutic for the one expressing, it also brings insight, comfort, and inspiration to those who experience or receive the work.

9. Physical Activity

Engaging in physical activity like sports, walking, running, or even punching a pillow can help release pent-up emotions stored in the body. Movement not only relieves stress but also produces endorphins, which can improve mood and promote emotional balance.

Chapter 5

WHY ARE THEY SO UNFAIR?

Camilla lost her father when he was just forty-five years old, and she was barely sixteen. While many people loss their parents, she often reflects that it was a different kind of pain when it happened so early, when one is still vulnerable, dependent and powerless.

Growing up within the traditional Idoma culture of Nigeria, she witnessed firsthand the cultural beliefs and practices that followed the death of a husband. In her community, there was a common, though deeply unjust, assumption that when a man died, his wife must have been responsible for his death. This belief brought with it a series of harsh treatments toward the widow, and in Camilla's case, the cruelty extended to her and her siblings.

Her mother, a young woman of thirty-five with six children, became the target of accusations and maltreatment from her late husband's family. Her father had come from a polygamous family, and his immediate younger brother who shared the same mother with him, was the one who led the campaign of hostility against them. Camilla recalled how, when her father, a military officer, died, his workplace was supposed to pay certain benefits to his immediate family. However, even before the funeral, her uncles began to show signs of greed and malice. Her father's colleagues noticed the tension and decided to delay payment until after the burial, hoping her mother would have regained her emotional stability. Later, her mother herself requested a further delay out of fear, as she was being threatened by her in-laws, who wanted to take control of everything her husband left behind.

The threats were severe. They accused her mother of killing her husband, threatened to force her to marry one of them, and even resorted to diabolical means to harm her, saying she would go mad. Ironically, Camilla later recounted that the uncle who had spearheaded these wicked acts ended up losing his own wife to madness, the very fate they had wished upon her mother.

Camilla remembered one particularly heated moment when she challenged her uncle about the way they were treating her family. The uncle told her bluntly that if not for the fact that her father had served in the military, and the force authorities were monitoring the situation, he would have taken her and her siblings to the village and stopped them from going to school.

Her uncles refused to have any cordial relationship with her mother or the children, and there was no support whatsoever from any of her father's relatives. Her mother carried the entire burden of raising six children alone. Whenever anyone tried to help, the uncles would spread false rumours that the person was her mother's lover, effectively isolating them from any potential support. In Idoma culture, such an accusation carried heavy stigma, and people avoided getting involved.

Camilla remembered how their once lively home, always full of relatives and friends when her father was alive, became desolate after his death. The isolation was crushing. Any time someone visited, they would fall to their knees to thank God for the company, as visits became rare and precious. If a visitor ever spent the night, it was an unforgettable event. Her uncles had succeeded in turning people against them, and the family lived in near-total social isolation.

Even years later, when Camilla got into the university, she noticed that people from her village who knew her family still avoided her. The stigma lingered. The loss of her father had not only taken away their protector and provider but had also stripped them of their sense of belonging.

It was, for Camilla, a period marked by pain, betrayal, and resilience. A chapter of her life that would forever shape how she understood grief, injustice, and survival. Although her mother's story was tragic, it is equally heroic. Married at a young age, she had her first child at seventeen and Camilla at nineteen, she was left widowed at thirty-five with six children to raise, and she still managed to raise them with her meagre salary as a primary school teacher. The loss of her husband and the ensuing hostility from his family left her deeply wounded but determined.

For Camilla, that chapter became the lens through which she understood grief, injustice, and survival. It taught her that mourning is not always met with mercy, that in some cultures, a woman's greatest tragedy can also become her biggest trial.

> *Mourning is not always met with mercy. In some cultures, a woman's greatest tragedy can also become her biggest trial.*

****

GRIEF IN THE LENS OF OUR PERSONALITY AND CULTURE

In processing grief as discussed in chapter three, psychologist William Worden (2010) described several mediators of mourning, one of which was personality variables. This mediator refers to how our individual traits such as coping style, attachment style, temperament, personal resilience, age, gender, and even our spiritual or cultural beliefs influence how we experience and manage loss.

The truth is that society often overlooks this. We tend to expect everyone to grieve in the same way, at the same pace, and with the same expressions. But grief is not a one-size-fits-all experience. When we impose our expectations on others by telling them how to cry, when to stop, or what to feel, we can wound them even more deeply than the loss itself.

Let's look at two of the most powerful influences on how we grieve: our personality and our culture.

Temperament: The Personal Lens of Grief

The same way our temperaments differ, our expressions of grief also differ. A quiet, introverted person may process grief inwardly, preferring solitude and reflection. They might not speak often about their pain or show much outward emotions. In fact, they may appear composed even when their heart is breaking. An extroverted person, on the other hand, might express grief outwardly, display a lot of emotions, talk openly about their feelings, or seek the company of others for comfort. Neither is better. Neither means one is hurting more deeply than the other. It's simply the way each person is wired.

When my daughter, Grace, died, everyone in my family grieved differently. Some cried easily and often, while others went silent, unable to speak about her for months. There was no "right" way among us, just different hearts processing pain through different personalities.

What matters most is that grief finds expression. As Pastor and author Rick Warren once said, "If I don't let it out in healthy ways, I'm going to let it out in unhealthy ways." Whether through tears, prayer, writing, music, or silence, we need to find safe outlets for sorrow. Grief that is locked inside can show up later as anxiety, depression, or even physical illness.

> *"If I don't let it out in healthy ways, I'm going to let it out in unhealthy ways."* - Rick Warren

Culture: The Collective Lens of Grief

Beyond personality, our culture also has a powerful say in how we mourn or how we are expected to mourn. In the African setting I come from, particularly among the Idoma tribe in Nigeria, grief is expected to be dramatic. You are not considered to be truly mourning until you have raised a loud, high-pitched song of lamentation when you arrive at the family house of the deceased. It is almost a performance, one that signals to others, "I am grieving."

When the death of a loved one is announced, it is customary for family members, relatives, friends, and neighbours to assemble at the deceased's residence, often before the arrival of the body. Each newcomer is expected to participate in a vocal lament, typically delivered in song, which is then joined by those already present. This tradition is observed regardless of an individual's personal connection to the deceased; it is noted that many mourners may draw upon personal memories of other losses to facilitate the outward expression, while verbally invoking the name of the departed. The mourning period may extend over several days or weeks prior to the funeral.

Culturally, individuals who do not engage in this expressive form of mourning are subject to criticism, with remarks such as, "It is surprising she did not cry at such a significant loss. Not even a tear or sound of lamentation was heard from her," commonly expressed. To avoid such criticism, many simply play along, performing grief to satisfy expectation rather than to express true feeling.

The original intention behind this may be to create community and shared emotion, which isn't bad. But it can also become a kind of emotional theatre, especially for people who don't naturally express grief that way. There are even cases where families hire professional mourners to heighten the emotional atmosphere.

As a naturally introverted person, I struggled with this. When my father died in 2016, I didn't do the dramatic wailing my relatives expected, and I could feel their disappointment. So, when my mother passed in 2019, an aunt decided to teach me how to mourn "properly." I tried, but it felt awkward and unnatural. I soon went back to my quiet way of grieving which meant crying quietly, remembering, and sitting in silence.

Over time, I learned something freeing: it's okay to mourn in your own way. You don't owe anyone a display. No one feels the pain of your loss more deeply than you do.

> *Culture may shape our mourning, but authenticity heals it.*

Culture may shape our mourning, but authenticity heals it.

THE ROLE OF CULTURE IN GRIEF

The experience of Camilla and her family remind us that while grief is universal, how we experience it is deeply shaped by who we are and where we come from. For her, grief wasn't only about losing her father, it was about being isolated from her community and losing her sense of belonging because of the impact of culture.

Culture and the Meaning of Loss

Culture doesn't just dictate how we mourn, it also shapes what we believe about death itself. Every society has stories that explain what happens after someone dies, and these beliefs profoundly influence how grief unfolds.

In many African traditions, death is not an end but a transition. The deceased become ancestors, believed to be still present, still influential, still part of the family's spiritual life. This belief can bring comfort and connection. In contrast, in more secular Western cultures, death is often viewed as final, and the focus shifts toward closure and emotional independence (Parkes, 1998).

Each of these perspectives frame grief differently and shape the way people find meaning and peace. Anthropologist Paul Rosenblatt (2008) notes that cultures teach their members how to interpret death by what to fear, what to hope for, and how to carry on.

When people grieve, they not only miss the person who passed, they are also trying to make sense of what has happened. Psychologist Colin Murray Parkes calls this the search for meaning, a key part of healing after loss. For those with strong cultural or spiritual beliefs, rituals and stories can fill that need. For others, meaning might come through memories, legacy, or personal transformation.

Rituals

Rituals are the heart of cultural grieving. They give structure to chaos. Whether it's a funeral, a wake, a memorial service, or periods of mourning, rituals serve to honour the dead and hold the living together.

Elisabeth Kübler-Ross (1969) and William Worden (2010) both emphasized that rituals help mourners move through, or work through their grief. They make loss visible and legitimate. When handled with care, rituals can provide comfort, connection, and closure.

But when misused, they can reinforce inequality and stigma. Across many parts of Nigeria and sub-Saharan Africa, the death of a husband does not only mark the beginning of grief for a widow, but it can also mark the beginning of real torture. What should be a period of mourning and healing is often transformed by culture into a painful ordeal. In these communities, a widow is not simply allowed to grieve her loss. Instead, suspicion follows her. People whisper that perhaps she had a hand in her husband's death, or that she carries some sort of spiritual stain from the tragedy. This widow might be forced to undergo "cleansing" rituals which sometimes involve drinking the water used to wash her husband's corpse. These practices are meant to prove her innocence or purify her from misfortune, but in reality, they strip her of dignity and humanity at the moment she most needs compassion.

The days that follow can be even harsher. A widow may be required to sit on the floor for weeks, shave her head, and remain confined indoors. She may need to dress in dark mourning cloth and be forbidden to cook, work, or even step outside her home. The intent, elders might say, is to honour tradition or show respect for the dead. Yet for many women, these customs bring more than sorrow; they bring economic hardship, isolation, and deep psychological wounds.

When a husband dies, his death can also mean the end of his wife's financial security. In some cultures, the man's property passes immediately to his family, leaving the widow without land, a home, or inheritance. What was once her shared household becomes someone else's possession overnight. In the most extreme cases, the widow herself becomes part of that inheritance as she is "taken" by a male relative of her late husband in what is known as widow inheritance or levirate marriage. Such arrangements, often made without her consent, can expose her to further emotional, sexual, and economic vulnerability.

Camilla's mother lived this reality. Her cultural community accused her of causing her husband's death and subjected her to cruel treatment under the guise of tradition. Instead of supporting her grief, culture became her oppressor. Yet her resilience, her refusal to accept the false blame, was itself an act of courage against oppressive tradition.

Emotional Expression and Cultural Expectations

Culture doesn't just tell us what to do after loss; it also tells us how to feel. In some societies, loud wailing and expressive crying are signs of love and respect. In others, quiet composure and private reflection are seen as more appropriate. I've met people who say, "I couldn't cry at the funeral because I didn't want to seem weak." That's culture at work.

Worden's theory of grief reminds us that there's no right or wrong way to mourn, but cultural norms can make people feel like they are "failing" at grief if they don't express it the "acceptable" way. Some feel pressured to "move on" quickly, while others feel obligated to mourn for years to prove their love. Understanding these expectations can help us be kinder, to ourselves and to others when grief looks different.

Culture, Power, and Gender

It's important to acknowledge that culture is not neutral. It often reflects the power structures within a society. Around the world, grief often exposes gender and social inequalities. Women, especially widows, are expected to mourn longer, louder, and more visibly than men. As I already mentioned, some traditions even subject them to purification rituals or deny them inheritance rights.

However, the men rarely face the same ordeal. When a wife dies, a widower may remarry quickly, and society may even encourage it. No one demands he sit in seclusion or shave his head. The contrast is stark: widowhood is treated as a social curse for women, but for men, it is merely a personal loss.

Beneath these culture and customs lies a web of patriarchy and power. Limited education and weak legal protection allow such practices to persist, even when they clearly violate human dignity. For many widows, the result is a loss not only of their spouse, but of their autonomy, self-worth, and place in society.

However, change has slowly begun to happen. Churches, NGOs, and advocacy groups are challenging these norms, urging communities to replace cruelty with compassion. Legal reforms and education programs are helping widows know and claim their rights, and economic empowerment initiatives are also allowing them to rebuild their lives after loss.

The path forward is not about rejecting culture but about re-defining it such that it transforms mourning from an instrument of suffering into an expression of love, solidarity, and healing.

Culture as a Source of Healing

Despite its complexities, culture can also be a tremendous source of healing. Rituals, faith traditions, and communal practices remind us that love doesn't end with death. Religious and spiritual beliefs, whether in eternal life, reincarnation, or ancestral presence, can help people hold on to hope.

Modern grief research supports this. Klass, Silverman, and Nickman (1996) introduced the idea of continuing bonds—maintaining a healthy, ongoing connection with the deceased through memories, prayer, or symbolic acts. Many cultural traditions have been doing this for centuries.

Culture, at its best, gives us ways to remember without despairing, to love without clinging, and to find belonging even in our pain.

Culture, at its best, gives us ways to remember without despairing, to love without clinging, and to find belonging even in our pain.

Culture and Community

One of the most beautiful aspects of culture is that it often builds community around grief. In many African and Asian contexts, loss is shared. Neighbours cook, pray, and sit with the bereaved for days or even weeks. The idea is simple but profound: no one should grieve alone. John Bowlby (1980) argued that the presence of supportive relationships is one of the most powerful buffers against the pain of loss.

Finding Balance

Culture shapes grief in both gentle and harsh ways. It teaches us how to honour the dead but sometimes forgets to protect the living.

When culture comforts, we should cherish it. When it wounds, we must challenge it.

When culture comforts, we should cherish it. When it wounds, we must challenge it.

Camilla's story reminds us that grief is not just a personal journey; it's also a cultural one. However, grief becomes healthier when we allow authenticity to guide us rather than social or cultural pressure. Healing often begins when we separate what is truly sacred from what is simply inherited.

In the end, each person must find their own balance between personality, tradition, and truth. Grief is both personal and cultural, but it is always human. Getting through it begins when we give ourselves permission to mourn, in our way.

CLOSING REFLECTIONS

As we close this chapter, we must recognise that culture plays a double-edged role in grief. On one hand, it offers structure, language, and meaning through rituals that help the bereaved navigate loss and find their footing in a time of chaos. On the other, it can reinforce inequality, perpetuate stigma, and turn mourning into suffering. Understanding this delicate balance is essential for anyone working in grief counselling, coaching, therapy, social work, or community leadership within culturally diverse societies. Grief should bring people together, not tear families apart. Culture should evolve to protect the vulnerable, not punish them.

Camilla's story challenges us to reflect deeply on how cultural norms shape our responses to death, and to ask whether compassion, rather than accusation, stands at the heart of our mourning traditions. Her experience reminds us that while culture can be a source of strength, it can also be an instrument of pain if left unquestioned.

In essence, culture acts as both a guide and a gatekeeper in the grieving process. It guides mourners through shared rituals and collective meanings that help them endure. Yet it also acts as a gatekeeper, deciding who is allowed to grieve, how, and for how long. Recognising this duality allows us to support others with empathy and cultural sensitivity. There is no single "right" way to mourn, but there is a right spirit, with compassion at its core.

There is no single "right" way to mourn, but there is a right spirit, with compassion at its core.

And finally, to cushion the harsh effects of culture in moments like those faced by Camilla's family, practical foresight becomes vital. Breadwinners should ensure that they leave clear wills, protecting their spouses and children from exploitation after their death. Husbands, in particular, should strive to empower their wives educationally, economically, and emotionally, so that they can stand on their own feet when life's storms inevitably come.

Only when compassion, justice, and preparation walk hand in hand with culture can mourning truly serve its purpose, which is to heal, to honour, and to hold families together in love.

Chapter 6

WHY DO I FEEL SHAME?

It was December 2022. The year was winding down, and Steve had begun to count his blessings, thanking God for provision, protection, and the quiet grace that had carried him and his family through another year. Then, on the 15th of December, the call came. His younger brother, Sam, the one who lived in the United Kingdom had been stabbed to death in a knife attack!

For a long moment, Steve simply stared at his phone, the words refusing to make sense. No, he thought, it must be a mistake. This is definitely a case of mistaken identity. Sam couldn't be dead. He had just spoken with him two days earlier, though the conversation had ended in sharp words. They had argued, and Steve had hung up with frustration in his voice. Now, that call replayed in his head like a broken record.

When a friend of Sam's, who lived in the same city, confirmed the news, the disbelief cracked open into something darker, guilt. A heavy, suffocating guilt that wrapped itself around his heart. He kept thinking: *Maybe if I'd prayed harder... Maybe if I hadn't argued with him... Maybe if I'd stopped him from traveling in the first place...* Every "maybe" was a knife twisting deeper.

Then came the shame. "I didn't know that death comes with shame," Steve said later, his voice hollow. His family was known for their faith. They were people who prayed, who trusted God openly. Now, every look from a neighbor felt like a question: You mean the God you always talk about couldn't save your brother?

And the manner of death! This was the hardest part to accept. Sam was murdered by gang members. The sort of tragedy you hear about on the news, shaking your head, thinking it happens to other people, but not to families like yours. Not to people with faith like yours. But it had come home. For days, Steve wished it had been anything else like an accident, an illness, anything but this brutal termination.

And as if grief were not enough, rumors began to spread. There were different conflicting stories. Some said Sam died in the middle of a gang clash, caught between two rival groups. Others claimed he was involved in drugs and killed when he couldn't pay the debt he had incurred from this lifestyle. Then came a third story that said Sam wasn't the target at all. He had been walking home from work when a fight broke out nearby, and a stray knife found him in the chaos. Although Steve didn't know which one was true, this third version looked more like the brother he knew because they had been raised with good values, but the other versions were the ones making the news headlines and going viral on social media. This was heartbreaking and shameful, and he began to hide.

He avoided church, skipped calls, and turned away from neighbours. The prayers that once brought him peace now felt heavy. He could not bring himself to pray to the God who had not protected his brother.

And in that silence, grief turned inward.

****

SHAME AND GRIEF

Shame doesn't always follow loss, but sometimes it does. And when it does, it's like a shadow that distorts everything it touches. It tells the grieving person, "You should have done more." It whispers, "People are judging you. Did you see the way that person looked at you?" Shame distorts your identity and makes you want to hide. It convinces you that your loss is evidence of failure on your part.

And for people of faith, this can be even heavier. If you believe in divine protection, tragedy can feel like divine abandonment. You begin to question your faith, your prayers, even your worthiness. Steve's story reveals this painful reality, where shame follows grief and distorts your identity and confidence. He wasn't just mourning his brother's death, he was mourning the loss of certainty, the belief that faith could keep tragedy away.

THE ORIGIN OF SHAME

The word "shame" comes from the old English word "scamu" or "sceomu," rooted in the Proto-Germanic "skamo" which relates to the concept of "covering" oneself, a common expression of shame. It also carries other meanings like "a painful feeling of guilt, state of being in disgrace; and loss of esteem or reputation." At its core, shame is a feeling of humiliation or embarrassment rooted in the sense that you have done something immoral, improper or dishonourable; or worse, that you yourself are fundamentally flawed. Shame can become extremely harmful when internalized and results in a harmful evaluation of yourself.

Common symptoms and behaviours of shame include:
- Hypersensitivity to what others think
- Feelings of rejection or inadequacy
- Withdrawal from people
- Silence, even when you have something meaningful to say
- Downward eye gaze
- Holding your head down and slumping the shoulders

- Covering your face or body
- Avoidant or closed posture

For Steve, shame showed itself in avoidance as he evaded people, places, and conversations that reminded him of his loss. It was not that he stopped believing in God; it was that he no longer felt the confidence he once had to talk to God boldly. Shame seemed to have tampered with both his self-confidence and his God-confidence. It muted his voice.

Human beings experience shame on multiple levels. It comes as emotional, relational, and spiritual all at once, which is why it can feel so overwhelming and so deeply rooted. Understanding its origins from these three perspectives of psychological, social, and spiritual, gives us language for what often feels like a wordless pain.

Psychological Origin: The Inner Mirror

Psychologically, shame is one of the earliest emotions we learn, not because someone teaches it to us, but because it naturally emerges as our self-awareness develops.

Developmental researchers such as Michael Lewis have shown that shame appears when a person is between eighteen months and two years old, around the time a child can recognise themselves in a mirror. This is the beginning of what psychologists call "self-conscious emotions,"

emotions that require a sense of self to exist. Shame, guilt, pride, and embarrassment all fall into this category.

Silvan Tomkins, one of the pioneers in the study of affect, described shame as a "sudden interruption of positive emotion." In other words, shame comes when something disrupts our sense of being accepted, connected, or "good." It is the emotional equivalent of a curtain dropping over the heart.

June Tangney, a leading shame researcher, explains that shame is fundamentally about identity. Guilt says: "I did something wrong." Shame says: "Something is wrong with me." This is why shame feels heavy and sticky, it attaches itself not to actions but to our identity.

Shame can both be healthy and unhealthy, and psychologically, this serves two purposes.

Healthy shame

Healthy shame is a normal and adaptive emotion that can act as a moral compass, helping us to see when we have done something wrong (e.g. telling a lie). In this healthy form, shame acts like a guardrail. It helps us stay connected to others by discouraging behaviours that might harm our relationships. This kind of shame is brief, corrective, and external, and it fades once behaviour is repaired.

Toxic shame

Toxic (or unhealthy) shame is when we allow ourselves to be defined by a perceived weakness or something we have no control over such as grief, trauma and abuse. It is internalized and becomes a lens through which we view ourselves. It tells us we are fundamentally unlovable, inadequate, or defective. This is the kind of shame that causes people to withdraw, hide their feelings, silence their voices, or avoid relationships altogether.

This was Steve's experience. His shame wasn't about something he had done. It was about who he suddenly felt he was, a brother who failed, a man whose prayers didn't "work," a Christian who couldn't protect his family. Toxic shame turns pain inward and convinces us that sorrow is proof of personal deficiency.

Social Origin: The Eyes of Others

Shame is not only internal, but also profoundly social. It is shaped by culture, community, and the expectations we absorb from the world around us. Sociologists like Erving Goffman have described shame as "a threat to one's social identity." It arises when we fear that others will see us as flawed or unacceptable. This is why shame thrives in secrecy; the moment we imagine ourselves exposed; we shrink.

Collectivist cultures

In collectivist societies, common in Africa, Asia, and parts of the Middle East, the individual and the family are deeply intertwined. What one person does reflects on everyone. In these contexts, shame becomes a tool for social harmony. Families may feel disgrace when a member struggles with addiction, divorce, financial ruin, or even grief that seems "too messy" or "too public." Their shame often comes from how others see them as they are very concerned with, "What will people think or say?"

Steve's story fits here. Being a Nigerian, his shame grew not only from his personal pain but from the perceived judgment of a community that associated strong faith with immunity from tragedy.

Individualistic cultures

In individualistic societies, shame often comes from failing personal ethics, not meeting a standard we set for ourselves. The message becomes: "I should have known better. I failed myself." Even then, the root is relational. We fear the loss of admiration, respect, or belonging.

Social shame in grief

Grief also carries its own social rules, unspoken expectations about how long grief should last, how visibly it should be expressed, and what losses "qualify" for sympathy. When people break these rules, shame follows.

Steve felt it every time someone avoided eye contact, every time a rumor surfaced about Sam's death, every time he imagined the whisper: "Where was their God?"

Shame grows in places where image matters, where reputation holds weight, and where suffering is interpreted as moral failure.

Spiritual/Theological Origin: The First Awareness of Nakedness

The deepest layer of shame is spiritual. In the Judeo-Christian tradition, the first appearance of shame occurs in Genesis chapter 3 verse 7, moments after Adam and Eve ate the forbidden fruit in the garden.

"Then the eyes of both of them were opened, and they realised they were naked; so they sewed fig leaves together and made coverings for themselves."[28]

Before this, they were "naked and they felt no ashamed."[27] Afterward, their immediate reaction was to hide, not only from each other, but from God. That moment they realised the need to hide, was the birth of shame and it reveals something profound: Shame enters when connection breaks. It is a human response to brokenness, to the fear of being seen, known, and fully exposed.

Theologically, shame's origin lies in four ruptures:

- Disconnection from God — "I must hide from Him."
- Disconnection from self — "Something is wrong with me."
- Disconnection from others — "They will reject me."
- Disconnection from identity — "I no longer know who I am."

Theologians often distinguish between guilt (a moral reality) and shame (a relational reality). Guilt says, "I violated God's law." Shame says, "I can no longer stand before God." This is why shame strikes at the very core of spiritual life. People stop praying, avoid sacred spaces, and begin to imagine God looking at them with disappointment rather than compassion.

Steve didn't stop believing in God. But he lost the confidence to approach Him. His prayers felt hollow not because God had changed, but because shame had altered his perception of himself.

****

Understanding shame from psychological, social, and spiritual angles helps us see its full complexity:

- Psychological shame attacks identity.
- Social shame attacks belonging.

- Spiritual shame attacks connection with God.

When all three are present, as they often are in trauma and grief, people feel lost, exposed, and voiceless. Knowing this allows us to move toward healing with compassion, clarity, and gentleness.

HEALING FROM SHAME

Shame is powerful, but it doesn't have to stay with you permanently. It may whisper that you are damaged, unworthy, or alone, but you must know that shame does not tell the truth. You can overcome shame and be healed from it, not in a moment, but through a gentle, deliberate process of reclaiming your identity, reconnecting to others, and returning to God with an open heart.

Healing from shame requires the opposite of what shame demands. Shame urges hiding; healing calls for courageous visibility. Shame isolates; healing restores connection. Shame says, "You are unworthy." God says, "You are loved."

Below are pathways that help you untangle the grip of shame and open the heart to wholeness again.

1. Bring Shame into the Light

Shame grows strongest in secrecy. It feeds on silence. Psychologist Brené Brown calls shame "a silent epidemic" because people rarely talk about it. The very nature of shame makes us want to hide, but the moment shame is spoken, even in a whisper, its power weakens. This doesn't mean sharing your heart with everyone. It means finding a safe person: a counselor, a trusted friend, a pastor, a spouse, or even writing to God in a journal.

When Steve finally opened up to one trusted friend, he later said, "I didn't know how much I was carrying until I heard myself say it out loud." Naming shame is the first step toward healing. You cannot heal what you hide.

2. Replace Self-Judgment with Compassion

Shame internalizes harsh judgment. It tells you what you should have done, who you should have been, how you failed the people you love. But healing begins when we learn to treat ourselves with the same compassion we readily offer others. Self-compassion is not self-pity. Psychologist Kristin Neff describes self-compassion as three things:

Healing begins when we learn to treat ourselves with the same compassion we readily offer others.

- Self-kindness — speaking to yourself gently, not harshly.
- Common humanity — remembering that suffering and imperfection are universal.
- Mindfulness — acknowledging your feelings without letting them define you.

A gentle question to ask yourself is: If someone I love experienced this, what would I say to them? Then say those words to yourself.

3. Challenge the False Story

Shame is not just a feeling; it is a story your mind constructs about who you are. And often, that story is incomplete, inaccurate, or absolutely false.

Shame told Steve:

- "You failed."
- "You should have prevented your brother's death."
- "Your prayers didn't work."
- "You are not a good Christian."

None of these were true but they felt true. Healing requires confronting the story shame tells, examining it, and rewriting it with truth and compassion. Cognitive behavioural techniques refer to this as "reframing." The same way that you can positively reframe your grief experience as I discussed in chapter four, you can also reframe the story that shame is trying to paint for you.

So, when shame is bombarding your mind with a narrative, you need to ask yourself:

- Is this thought true?
- Is it kind?

Healing requires confronting the story shame tells, examining it, and rewriting it with truth and compassion.

- Is it helpful?
- Would I say this to someone else?

And if your answer to any of these questions is a "No," then you will need to reframe that story. Any belief that diminishes your identity, your dignity, or your worth does not deserve a permanent place in your heart.

4. Reconnect With Safe Community

Shame isolates but healing flourishes in connection. No matter how difficult it might be, make every effort to reconnect with a safe community. In healthy, supportive relationships, your identity will be mirrored back to you in truth instead of the distortion that shame presents. Love has a way of helping you see yourself clearly again.

Reconnecting with community does not mean showing up and pretending to be strong. It simply means showing up in your humanity. For some, this means returning to church after a painful season. For others, it means joining a grief support group or inviting one trusted friend back into your everyday life. Healing happens when someone looks at you, in your grief, in your bruised identity and still says, "You belong."

5. Engage the Body

Shame is not just emotional; it is physical. It lives in slumped shoulders, downward gazes, clenched stomachs, and tight chests. This means healing must also involve the body.

The following gentle practices can help release stored shame:

- deep breathing
- walking in nature
- stretching
- grounding techniques
- somatic exercises
- writing while paying attention to bodily sensations

Even lifting your chin and opening your posture can shift your internal experience, giving small signals to your nervous system that you are safe enough to be seen.

6. Restore Your Connection with God

If you are a person of faith like Steve, shame can create a disconnect between you and God. It makes you believe that you are too flawed, too broken, too guilty to stand before God. It convinces you that God is disappointed in you, or that He has withdrawn His presence. Yet Scripture paints a different picture, one of God walking through the garden and calling, "Where are you?"

Not in anger, but in longing.

And God covers Adam and Eve with garments, even after their failure, symbolising that He meets shame with compassion. Healing spiritually means coming out of hiding, even with trembling hands, and allowing God to meet you where you are. This may involve whispering small, honest prayers, reading the Word, listening to worship music, journaling your anger, questions, and confusion, or simply sitting in silence and letting yourself be held by God's presence.

Shame says, "Don't pray."

Grace says, "Come as you are."

7. Integrate Grief and Identity

Shame often tells you that your loss defines you:

- You are the one whose brother was murdered.
- You are the one whose faith didn't work.
- You are the one who should have done more.

But healing means reclaiming your identity, integrating grief into your story without letting it become the whole story. You can continue to evolve and rediscover yourself, and this will make your story more powerful and inspiring. This is what I have done and continue to do after the loss of my daughter.

- You can grieve and still be faithful.
- You can ache and still be loved.
- You can question and still belong to God.

You will never forget your loss, but as you heal, you can remember it truthfully, without letting shame rewrite who you are.

DEVELOPING SHAME RESILIENCE

The journey of recovering from shame is like that of recovering from grief and it is not linear. It takes time, compassion, courage, and community. Some days you will feel strong. Other days, you may feel like hiding again. But you can develop resilience to shame that fosters your healing. The truth is, shame may have a loud voice, but it does not have to get the final word.

You can develop shame resilience by:

i. Recognising shame and understanding its triggers. These are often hidden in other painful emotions, such as blame and fear, hence making the triggers go unnoticed, and this can cause you to react in ways that exacerbate shame. Learning to recognise the physical signs of shame that I have already discussed earlier in this chapter, and its triggers, can help us navigate the emotion better.

ii. Practicing critical awareness: The expectations driving shame are often unrealistic and unattainable. Practicing critical awareness allows us to understand why these expectations exist and what they impact.

iii. Reaching out: Connection is a vital element of shame resilience. It enables us not only to experience empathy but also allows us to feel valued, affirmed, and accepted.

iv.   Speaking shame: When we feel shame, we must learn to ask what we need or risk entering a shame spiral.

Steve's Return

Months passed before Steve walked through the doors of his church again. For a long time, every Sunday morning, he watched from the balcony of his apartment as people streamed to church. He missed community, but the thought of stepping into it made his heart pound. He still feared the looks, the questions, the silent pity as shame still clung to him like a heavy cloak.

After much encouragement from one of his friends, he decided to go with him to church about three months down the line. To Steve's amazement, when they entered the building which already had people seated, no one stared, no one whispered. A few people nodded with genuine affection, some hugged him, and others simply touched his shoulder as they passed, wordless but comforting. The world he had imagined as judgmental felt, instead, quietly welcoming, and for the first time in months, he felt the faint warmth of belonging.

During worship, Steve couldn't sing. His throat closed and tears threatened to choke him. He bowed his head, overwhelmed by a mixture of grief and the unfamiliar gentleness of being seen without being scrutinised. As the music filled the room, he felt a whisper in his heart, not loud, not dramatic, but unmistakably tender:

"You're home."

It wasn't the church building that made him feel that way; it was the sense of connection he had been afraid to seek. It was the reminder that God had not abandoned him, shame had simply blinded him to God's nearness.

After the service, someone asked softly, "How are you doing, Steve?"

Not the casual greeting people exchange in passing, but the kind of question that invites honesty. He hesitated, then answered with a shaky exhale:

"I'm not okay... but I'm here."

It was the truest thing he had said in months.

The man nodded. "That's enough for today."

And somehow, it was.

That day marked the beginning of Steve's slow return, not just to church, but to himself. He began meeting with a counselor who helped him untangle the knots of grief and shame. He started to talk more and have deep conversations with George, his close friend who chose not to leave him alone during those dark moments of his life. He started to pray again, they were short, imperfect prayers and sometimes he didn't have words, just tears. But gradually, the heaviness in his chest loosened. Shame didn't disappear all at once. But its grip weakened.

- It loosened each time he told his story without trying to hide.
- It loosened each time someone responded with compassion instead of the judgment he feared.
- It loosened each time he remembered that tragedy was not a reflection of his worth or a measure of his faith.

> *Tragedy is not a reflection of your worth or a measure of your faith.*

He still missed his brother deeply. But the shame that once smothered his grief no longer defined his story. He had re-entered community. He had rediscovered his voice. And slowly, he had found his way back to hope.

He now knows that you can grieve without drowning in shame.

Chapter 7
WHY DO I FEEL GUILTY MOVING FORWARD?

Angela and her husband, Josh, married and had their children when they were still quite young. For years their life revolved around changing diapers, school runs, packed lunches, and the constant shuttle of children's activities. They loved their family, but they also longed for the day the kids would grow up, when the house would finally quiet down and they could rediscover each other not just as parents, but as partners.

They dreamed of long weekends away, of slow mornings, of dinner dates that didn't require bribing or begging anyone to babysit. It was the life they believed they had earned after years of sacrifice. But just as that long-awaited season approached, something shifted. Josh began to experience vague discomfort, nothing dramatic, just "off" days that came and went. He would say, "Something doesn't feel right," but by the next morning he seemed fine again. The ambiguity made them believe it wasn't anything serious until the diagnosis finally came in May 2017. It was stage four colon cancer! The diagnosis felt impossible.

How? Why? What did they miss?

The quiet dreams they had been nurturing suddenly shattered.

Over the next months, Josh's health declined sharply. Chemotherapy drained him, his hair fell out, his weight dropped, his energy evaporated. But Angela clung to hope as she prayed fiercely, clinging to every scripture on healing she had ever known. She believed Josh would recover but in December 2018, eighteen months after the diagnosis, he died.

As Angela grieved the passing of her husband, she found herself being consumed with guilt. It settled in unnoticed at first, taking shape through questions she had no answers for.

Why didn't I insist he go to the doctor sooner?

Why didn't I take those early symptoms seriously?

What if we had caught it earlier?

What if—what if—what if...?

The guilt shaped her grief more sharply than the sorrow itself. It was not simply grief for the husband she lost, but grief for the actions she could not go back and take. It haunted her silently, in the same spaces where she used to feel his presence.

And beneath all of it lay a deeper, unspoken truth, she was also angry with God. She didn't realise the depth of that anger until one Sunday in church. When the pastor asked,

"How many of you know God is a healer?"

she felt her heart respond, "No, He isn't. He didn't heal my husband."

The thought startled her. It exposed the fracture grief had carved inside her faith. And the guilt kept circling back. She felt guilty for the anger, guilty for doubting God, and guilty for wanting a different future.

She realised that even when you see the death of a loved one coming, as with her husband gradually dying of cancer, grief can still be very devastating; especially when guilt is the lens through which every memory is replayed. As Angela processed her grief, she learned that nothing she did

> *Guilt cannot change anything, but it could destroy you if you let it.*

could change the past. She did her best with what she knew. She loved her husband deeply, but she now knows that Guilt cannot change anything, but it could destroy her if she let it.

She recalled how after his death, she would reach for her phone to text him about her day, only to freeze mid-sentence, realising there was no one on the other end. While reclining on her couch and watching a show, she would instinctively turn to say, "Did you see that?" before remembering that he was not there beside her, it was just an empty space. Through counselling, the passage of time, and the gradual restoration of her relationship with God, Angela began to release guilt's hold and find healing, until grief knocked at her door again.

****

A year and a half after Josh's death, in the middle of the pandemic in 2020, Angela returned home from church after helping her pastor set up new camera equipment. She took a walk with a friend, grabbed some food, and pulled into her driveway, immediately noticing her son Dan's car was missing. She made a mental note to call him later to tell him he needed to come home because they were going to her brother's house the next day.

Moments later, there was a knock at her door. Her son's friend's brother stood there, saying,

"The boys got into a car wreck, but they're fine."

But Angela didn't believe the reassurance. If they're fine, why isn't he here?

She rushed to the hospital and was shocked when she saw her son. Even though he was still alive when she got there, he lay unconscious, swollen, connected to machines, and non-responsive. The shock was too much for her mind to process.

"This isn't "fine." This isn't even close to fine." She said repeatedly to herself.

As she stood there, staring at the stillness of his body, a part of her heart went silent. She prayed, bargained, and pleaded for his life to be spared. But a few days later, her twenty-year-old son died.

And guilt returned, but this time, it took a different form. It was the guilt of motherhood. A guilt that was so deep, instinctive, irrational and yet relentless.

I should have hugged him more.

I shouldn't have fussed at him.

I should have prayed over him before he left.

I should have done something, anything!

The pain was unbearable. "I can't do this again," she cried. "I am not built for this."

In the days that followed Dan's death, Angela wrestled not only with grief and guilt, but with the very idea of healing. She had always believed that when God heals, He does so in this world, in this body, in this lifetime. But as she prayed and sat in the crushing silence, another possibility emerged, one that was both painful and strangely comforting.

- What if healing doesn't always happen here?
- What if healing is stepping into the presence of Jesus?

- And what if, once someone experiences that glory, they never want to return?

Angela believed this was true for Dan, and it became the one thought that comforted her. If her son had truly met Jesus, he would not choose to come back to the brokenness of this world, not even for her. This revelation didn't erase her pain, but it wrapped her grief in a quiet peace, lessened the questions she asked, and loosened guilt's grip. It reminded her that love does not end, and neither does life.

Counseling helped her process the trauma, but faith, this new understanding of healing became the anchor she clung to.

"I don't know how people get through grief without God," she often says. "I certainly can't."

She thinks of her son often. Sometimes she cries without warning. But most days, she smiles at the baby picture on her desk, imagining how he'd laugh at a joke or what he'd think of something she's experiencing.

His loss left a different emptiness from her husband's, not the loss of partnership and protection, but the loss of light, of joy, of a gentle presence that brightened rooms without trying.

****

It took Angela three years after her husband's death before she could clean out his closet. She left his side untouched, just as he had left it, as though preserving it might anchor her to something solid. And then one morning, without any warning, she woke with the quiet certainty that she was ready. She cleaned out his closet and gave everything away without tears, guilt, or hesitation. She realised that this was a sign that healing had finally taken root. As she healed, she found herself transformed. She became more compassionate and less judgmental.

She remarried about six years after Josh's passing. Where she once criticized people for moving into new relationships quickly after loss, she now understood the raw hunger for companionship, the longing to fill the silence grief leaves behind. She recognised that people do not replace those they lose; they seek warmth in the cold spaces loss creates.

****

GRIEF AND GUILT

Guilt is one of grief's quietest and most persistent companions, and this is why It was added to the original Kübler-Ross five stages of grief to create the modified seven stages of grief. Studies show that nearly seventy percent of bereaved people experience some form of guilt, whether it's about what they did, what they didn't do, or what they wish they had known at the time.

When guilt shows up in grief, it makes its victim feel distressed or responsible for the bad situation because they think or feel they have violated a moral standard or failed to act when they should have done so. It often leads to remorse, regret, or shame, though oftentimes it stems from perceived, rather than actual wrongdoing.

Guilt doesn't always enter with a shout; often it slips in through the cracks, through unanswered questions, rewound memories, regrets that surface in the quiet hours of the night. Angela's story shows us just how deeply guilt can intertwine with loss. But her experience is not unique. Many grieving people find that guilt can become heavier than even the grief itself.

In the last chapter, I discussed how shame shows up in grief, but guilt is different from shame. Whereas shame is the feeling that one is inherently a bad person ("I am bad"), guilt focuses on a specific behaviour ("What I did or didn't do was very bad").

To understand why people feel guilty after a bereavement, and even more guilty moving forward, we must look beneath the surface into the psychology of loss, the biology of trauma, and the spiritual ache that death creates. Guilt in grief is rarely rational. It is almost always emotional, instinctive, and rooted in a longing to rewrite what cannot be rewritten.

WHY DO PEOPLE FEEL GUILTY?

Apart from the initial guilt of actions or inactions that could have caused the death of a loved one, many people also feel guilty for wanting to heal and be happy again, and here are some of the main reasons for this guilt:

1. The brain searches for control in the midst of chaos

When someone dies, especially unexpectedly or prematurely, the brain struggles with the overwhelming truth that we are not in control. Guilt becomes the mind's attempt to make sense of the senseless. In doing so, the brain protects the bereaved from the terror of helplessness because they believe that they could prevent the unpreventable in the future.

2. Fear of "forgetting" the person

People often feel that if they heal, laugh again, or open themselves up to new experiences, it means the person they lost is being left behind. Grief can create a sense that pain is the last tie to the person, so letting go of the pain feels like letting go of them.

3. Loyalty to the loved one

Grief can get tangled with a sense of loyalty where the bereaved person thinks, "If I still hurt, then it shows how much they mattered." Moving forward, which could mean laughing again, dreaming again, dating again, can feel like disloyal, as if the person is being replaced or their memory minimized. The person may be asking,

"If I smile, does it mean I didn't love them enough?"

"If I remarry, am I replacing them?"

"If I enjoy life, does that diminish their memory?"

4. We are wired to protect those we love

As humans, we are naturally wired to protect those we love, and this instinct can be especially higher in parents and spouses. So, when we lose a child or a partner, the protector in us feels like it has failed. Even when the death is beyond our control, our heart tells a different story. We think, "If I had done more, they'd still be here," and we wallow in guilt.

5. Identity shifts

Losing someone often changes how a person sees themselves for example as a parent, partner, child, sibling, or friend. Moving forward can feel like stepping into a new identity that no longer includes the dead person, and this can be scary or feel wrong.

6. Social pressure or expectations

People receive mixed messages from society. One day someone is telling you, "Take all the time you need." And the next day, another person tells you, "It's been long enough. It's high time you move on." This confusion can create guilt no matter what someone does.

7. Misunderstanding what "moving on" actually means

Many understand "moving on" as forgetting, replacing, or no longer loving the person. In reality, healthy grieving is about learning to carry the loss while still engaging in life. But until that truth sinks in, guilt can fill the space.

8. Trauma or unresolved grief

If the loss was sudden, complicated, or traumatic, people may feel stuck between wanting relief from pain and feeling obligated to stay in it. That conflict often shows up as guilt.

9. Spiritual expectations can intensify guilt

People of faith often wrestle with guilt of not praying enough, praying in ways that didn't "work" and guilt for being angry at God. Many quietly ask: "Is my loss a sign that my faith is weak?"

Angela's moment in church when her heart whispered, "No, He didn't heal my husband," is a moment countless grieving believers experience but rarely say aloud.

HOW TO DEAL WITH THE GUILT

When we truly understand the psychology of guilt, it can become easier to slowly release it and heal. We must remember that healing is not betrayal. It is not the end of love but rather the continuation of it.

Here are the ways people can begin to heal:

1. Identify what is true and what is emotional

Guilt stems more from emotions than facts. Grief psychologists have distinguished between Cognitive guilt and Emotional guilt. Cognitive guilt is guilt based on facts, while emotional guilt is guilt based on feelings, fear, or hindsight. Emotional guilt is "retroactive responsibility" where you blame yourself with information you did not have before the loss happened. You must remember that responsibility must be measured with the knowledge, resources, and circumstances you had then, not with the painful clarity you have now.

The University of Memphis Bereavement Lab found that hindsight bias dramatically amplifies guilt after trauma. People assume they "should have known," even when there was no reasonable way to know. So, when you ask yourself,

"Is this guilt based on fact or fear?"

"Did I truly do something wrong, or am I grieving what I wish I could have done?"

And when you know in your heart that this guilt is emotional not cognitive, then it would be helpful to write and say this out loud to yourself, "I made the best decisions I could with the information I had at the time." You may need to say this over and over again until you retrain your brain to align with truth rather than fear.

2. Speak the guilt out loud

Guilt thrives in silence and isolation but shrinks when spoken. Dr. Robert Neimeyer's research in grief counselling reveals that shame and guilt lose power when they are shared in safe environments. Speaking it reduces self-blame, offers perspective, interrupts distorted thinking, and help regulate the emotional brain. You can do this speaking about your guilt with a trusted friend, counsellor, therapist, coach, pastor, or even a grief support group.

Angela's relationship with her counsellor was a major turning point because guilt that is named becomes guilt that can be healed.

> *Guilt that is named becomes guilt that can be healed.*

3. Offer compassion to yourself—the kind you would give someone else

Cognitive-behavioural therapy (CBT), widely used in grief work, teaches that guilt often comes from distorted thinking patterns causing us to judge ourselves very harshly. Even though these thoughts seem to be automatic, you must remember that they are not accurate. So, it helps when you ask yourself,

- "Am I judging myself with standards no one could meet?"
- "If someone I loved experienced the exact same situation, would I blame them?

Almost always, the answer is no. Then extend the same compassion to yourself. In the self-compassion research done by Dr. Kristin Neff, it was shown that self-kindness reduces guilt and shame more effectively than positive thinking or distractions.

4. Make meaning from the loss

Dr. Robert Neimeyer's research done through the Meaning Reconstruction Model shows that healing accelerates when people find meaning after loss, not meaning in the death itself, but in the life that continues.

Angela's understanding of healing, especially her belief about eternal healing helped her reconstruct meaning after her son's death and release guilt.

So, it helps when you ask yourself, "How can my loved one's life shape the way I live now?" The answer to this question can transform guilt into purpose.

5. Give the loved one a place in your present

Even though holding on to guilt can feel like loyalty, it is healthier for you to integrate your loss into your life rather than clinging to suffering. Integration means you allow the person's life to remain part of your story without letting guilt dominate the narrative. This can be through telling their stories, keeping something meaningful (such as their photo) that represents the relationship, carrying their values, honouring their memory, allowing them to shape the person you've become. This transforms guilt into gratitude. Angela demonstrated this when she said, she smiles when she looks at Dan's baby picture on her desk.

6. Lean into spiritual anchors

Spiritual beliefs can either intensify guilt or bring profound relief. We saw both play out in Angela's life. Research from the Journal of Palliative Care finds that people who can reinterpret loss through their faith experience lower levels of guilt and complicated grief.

For Angela, the revelation that healing sometimes happens in eternity rather than on earth gave her peace, perspective and permission to release self-blame. Each person's spiritual understanding will be different, but faith offers two things grief desperately needs: meaning and hope, and both are antidotes to guilt.

For people of faith, I have found that it helps when you are able to get a personal word or revelation about your situation in your time of prayer, worship or study of scriptures. This will anchor your faith and help reframe guilt through the lens of grace.

7. Redefine what moving forward means

Moving forward does not mean forgetting, replacing, abandoning, dishonouring or necessarily "getting over it." It means learning to carry the loss with love, not with punishment.

Allow your heart to hold these two truths at the same time:

- You can miss them and still want to live.

- You can love them and still love again.

- You can grieve what happened and still hope for what is ahead.

8. Let healing happen in its time

There will come a moment, that quiet, surprising, and gentle moment when the heart realises it is ready to breathe again. For Angela, it was the morning she could finally clean her husband's closet with no guilt and no tears. Everyone has a moment like that, and when it comes,

> *You can learn to live in a way that honours both their memory and your future.*

don't suppress it. Allow yourself to live again. It is not betrayal, it is resurrection. You can learn to live in a way that honours both their memory and your future.

WHEN GUILT LOOSENS ITS GRIP

Guilt may enter our grief quietly, but it rarely leaves without a deliberate, courageous choice. It threads itself through our memories, our faith, our identity, and our longing for the life we once imagined. For many, guilt becomes the shadow grief casts over the heart, insisting that we should have known, should have seen, should have done something. Anything.

Angela's story reminds us that guilt does not appear because we failed. It appears because we loved. It is the mind's attempt to rewrite the past and the heart's attempt to hold on to what was lost. For a time, guilt may feel like the only connection to the person who is no longer here. It may feel like loyalty, or even the last remaining expression of care. But as Angela learned, guilt is a heavy burden to carry through the valley of grief. And it is a burden we were never meant to bear alone.

As she discovered through counseling, faith, and honest lament; guilt cannot change what happened, but it can change you, if you allow it to take root. It can steal your joy, distort your memories, and hinder your healing. But when you face it with truth, compassion, and the gentle presence of God, guilt begins to loosen its grip. It becomes something you can examine, understand, and ultimately, release.

Healing does not arrive in a single moment but unfolds slowly, in the morning you wake up with a little more peace than the day before, in the courage to face a memory without collapsing, in the ability to laugh without feeling disloyal. Healing is the moment you realise guilt is no longer your companion, but love that is unburdened and unpunished takes its rightful place in your life.

You do not honour the one you lost by staying wounded. You honour them by living in a way that reflects the love you shared.

Moving forward is not betrayal. It is the testimony of your

> *You do not honour the one you lost by staying wounded.*

resilience, of survival, and it deserves to be celebrated. It ends a chapter, but it never ends the story. Your story is still unfolding. And guilt is not the author.

As you turn the page of your own grief, may you find the courage to release what was never yours to carry, and embrace the life that still calls your name.

Chapter 8

WILL THIS PAIN EVER GO AWAY?

Oscar still remembers the weight of that morning in June 2021, the kind of weight that settles into a man's chest and never seems to fully leave.

Jonny was born in August 2007 and even though it had been almost fourteen years since his birth, the memory of his first months still played in Oscar's mind like yesterday. Jonny had arrived quietly into the world, an innocent child with a smile that would later light up rooms. But barely two months after his birth, the doctors spoke words Oscar had never heard before: They said Jonny had a hole in the heart! It was a sentence that sounded clinical and distant until it became deeply personal.

Oscar believed it would be fixed. "Surely this was something medicine could handle," he thought until he realised the magnitude of the condition. He and his wife prayed and hoped for the best and then came an opportunity to take Jonny to the United States. His treatment would be sponsored by a non-profit organization.

Oscar took this as confirmation that healing was on the way. But after several months in America, doing various tests and waiting, the doctors said what no parent is ever prepared to hear: performing a heart surgery on Jonny was too risky. He had failed all the major tests ran on him and his survival rate was Fifty–fifty. And because they wouldn't want to take such a chance, they decided not to proceed.

Oscar returned home disappointed but also in faith. If medicine could not help, then maybe God would show Himself in another way. And for fourteen years, He did. Jonny grew, not like a fragile child, but like a boy full of life. He ran, played football, rode bicycles, and laughed loudly. These were things he was not expected to do given his condition. He even went to a boarding school. He lived as if his heart was whole! The doctors were amazed.

At Jonny's birth, they had predicted he might not live beyond six months yet here he was at fourteen, having never suffered a single crisis. There was never a frantic rush to the hospital, never a moment when he needed oxygen to survive. To Oscar and his wife, there was only one explanation: a miracle had taken place.

The future looked bright until one morning in June 2021 when Oscar received a call from the school that Jonny was sick, his leg swollen, and he wasn't breathing well. He was quickly taken to the hospital, and after running tests, the result came out that his heart had failed. Oscar and his wife still prayed and hoped for a miracle but after some days of struggling in this condition, Jonny quietly died.

Oscar was devastated. He saw his son going and yet he could do nothing about it. He walked away and cried bitterly. The kind of cry that breaks something deep inside a man.

As at the time of writing this book and chatting with Oscar, it's been more than four years since the passing of Jonny, but Oscar still grieves for his son. Some days, he wakes up and the pain feels fresh, and tears well up. And other days, he fondly remembers Jonny for the fun moments they had spent together, his disciplined lifestyle and his leadership, especially in the way he guided his younger brother, and he's just grateful for the time they had with him.

Oscar believes he is making good progress in his healing journey as the intensity of the grief seem to be reducing but he still asks God for help. And when the pain becomes overwhelming, he remembers the quiet voice he once heard in the night:

Be calm.

Not because the pain disappeared, but because healing means learning how to slowly breathe again while carrying love, loss, and hope in the same heart.

****

Healing is a multifaceted process of becoming whole again, involving the body's natural repair of injury, restoration of mind-body-spirit balance, and finding meaning in suffering

If you are asking, "Will this pain ever go away?" you are not alone. Grief has a way of making that question echo in the quiet moments like early mornings, those nights that you are unable to sleep, and when unexpected reminders pop up. Grief does not follow rules neither does it respect time. And the pain does not disappear simply because you wish it would.

The honest answer is this: the pain may not completely go away, but it's intensity can reduce. At first, that truth can feel unsettling because we want an ending, a finish line, a day when it no longer hurts. But stay with me, because this is not the end of the story.

Yes, healing is possible. Just not in the way most grieving people expect.

Oscar's story and my own, help us understand this more clearly.

1. Healing is a journey, not a moment

For Oscar, healing did not arrive suddenly. Four years after losing Jonny, the ache is still present. Certain dates still sting. Seeing Jonny's classmates still reopens old wounds and reminds him of the life his son never lived. Yet something is changing. Healing is gradually taking root.

Healing has not completely removed the pain, but it has softened it and taught him how to live with it.

Healing from grief is not the absence of pain; it is the ability to carry the pain without being destroyed by it.

His story shows us that healing from grief is not the total absence of pain; it is the ability to carry the pain without being destroyed by it.

In Oscar's life, the healing journey looks like:

- Being able to speak about Jonny without breaking down in tears
- Turning toward God instead of away from Him when grief resurfaces
- Finding room for gratitude alongside loss when he remembers that "I still have other children"
- Learning to interrupt despair when it tries to hijack the day by practicing positive reframing
- Holding onto a simple statement, "Be calm," and letting it steady his soul

Oscar did not "get over" his son. A parent never does. But he moved forward. He learned how to carry grief without allowing it to define every moment of his life. That is healing in progress.

2. Healing is relinquishing control

Grief changes you. It reshapes how you see God, life, fairness, and control. Oscar once believed healing was a tangible miracle that everyone could see. But his experience has unfolded a perspective of healing he never knew —that healing came in surrender. Accepting that some questions may never have answers, and some prayers are met with presence rather than explanations.

Healing begins when you stop fighting what grief has changed and start growing within it. It unfolds slowly, unevenly, and often quietly. Some days you feel strong. Other days you feel fragile. Both can exist at the same time, and both are part of healing.

3. Healing is finding and making meaning

Healing is not erasing the past; it is integrating it into our present life. It is finding meaning without minimizing loss. Oscar began to find meaning not in why Jonny died, but in how Jonny lived. In the years he was given and in the love that shaped their family. And Jonny's life has made him more empathetic towards vulnerable children and birthed the dream to one day start a foundation that helps children with heart conditions.

Healing is not returning to who you were before, but becoming someone who can still hope, love, and breathe again.

4. Healing is not forgetting

Healing does not mean forgetting the one you lost. It does not mean the longing disappears or that certain days won't still hurt. Oscar still remembers Jonny when he sees his peers graduate, move forward, and begin new chapters. You will always remember the people you loved even after they are gone but you must remember that memory is not the enemy of healing. You remember because you loved, and love is the reason grief exists at all.

5. Healing is when the pain no longer controls you

Healing means learning how to wake up on hard days and still choose to live. It means discovering that your heart can hold grief and gratitude at the same time. It means finding the strength to breathe through the ache instead of being crushed by it. We see Oscar live this out when he chooses to focus on the positives in his life rather than the losses.

You may never be the person you were before the loss, but you can become someone who still hopes, still loves, and still finds meaning again.

6. Healing is wholeness

Healing ultimately leads to wholeness, a place of inner balance and peace.

From my own experience of losing my daughter, I learned this in a deeply personal way. For the first four years after her passing, my heart broke anew each time her death anniversary came around. The anguish was overwhelming, familiar, and heavy. But something unexpected happened in the fifth year. I woke up on her anniversary with a peace I couldn't explain. The sharp anguish that used to consume me was no longer there.

The loss was still real. The love was still present. But the pain no longer ruled my heart. At that moment, I knew something had shifted. My healing had moved into another level, a level of peace and wholeness. That peace did not mean I stopped missing her. It meant my soul had found balance again.

There will come a time when the memories don't only bring tears, but they also bring smiles. When the weight eases just enough for you to stand upright again. When you realise you are still here, still breathing, still moving forward, while carrying love, loss, and faith together.

HOW TO KICKSTART YOUR GRIEF HEALING PROCESS

One of the greatest misconceptions about grief is the belief that avoiding pain will make it go away. Many of us were taught directly or indirectly, to be strong, move on, or not dwell on it. While these responses may be well-intentioned, they often do more harm than good.

Healing from grief is not enhanced by avoidance, it is enhanced when we face our grief, process it, and allow it to do its work. Grief that is ignored does not disappear; it simply goes underground and

> *Healing from grief is not enhanced by avoidance, it is enhanced when we face our grief, process it, and allow it to do its work.*

waits. And when it resurfaces, it often shows up in unexpected ways: emotional numbness, chronic anger, anxiety, physical exhaustion, spiritual confusion, or a quiet sense of

Avoidance often postpones pain rather than prevents it.

disconnection from life. So, avoidance often postpones pain rather than prevents it.

Healing Begins When We Face Our Grief

Facing grief means acknowledging the loss, allowing yourself to feel what you feel, and giving yourself permission to mourn without shame. Facing grief is an act of courage not weakness, and it gives pain a voice. Grief needs expression because when pain is silenced, it becomes heavier. When it is named, it becomes manageable.

Oscar's story illustrates this truth clearly. He did not pretend his son never existed. He spoke about him. He allowed himself to feel the ache when memories returned. He acknowledged the pain instead of silencing it. That honesty became a doorway to healing.

Facing grief does not mean drowning in it, it simply means giving it a voice.

Processing Grief Allows Healing to Take Root

Grief must be processed, not suppressed. Processing does not mean obsessing over the loss; it means allowing the pain to move instead of stagnating. This happens through talking, crying, praying, remembering, journaling, or sitting quietly with God. Grief begins to change form as you process it and what once felt overwhelming slowly becomes bearable.

Oscar processed his grief by:

- Talking about Jonny openly with his wife and children instead of burying his memory
- Acknowledging difficult days instead of pretending they didn't exist
- Turning to God honestly, not with rehearsed words but with desperate cries for help
- Allowing the Holy Spirit to meet him in his weakness

This processing did not erase the loss, but it prevented the grief from hardening into despair.

Avoided grief often becomes complicated grief. Processed grief becomes integrated grief, which is woven into life rather than fighting against it.

Avoidance Delays Healing and Fragments the Soul

Avoidance often masquerades as busyness, spiritual clichés, excessive work, emotional shutdown, or even forced positivity. We tell ourselves we are "fine." But healing cannot take place in denial. True healing leads to wholeness, and wholeness requires honesty.

I learned this truth personally from my own experience of losing my daughter. Even though the pain was intense at the initial period and when her death anniversary came around, I did not run from it. I faced it, year after year until that fifth anniversary, when the overwhelming anguish was gone, and I found myself in a place of peace and wholeness. That peace which came naturally and not forcefully, was because I allowed myself to walk through the grief.

Let Faith Be a Safe Place to Process Grief

Some people believe that faith should shield us from grief. But faith was never meant to silence sorrow; it was meant to sustain us through it. The Psalms are filled with lament, questions, and tears. Even Jesus wept.

Oscar's healing deepened not because he suppressed his pain, but because he consistently brought it to God. When he reached the limits of his strength, he asked for help, and God met him with a simple but powerful word: Be calm.

That word did not erase the loss, but it anchored his soul. That is what facing grief with faith looks like.

What We Face, We Can Heal From

Healing from grief means the pain no longer controls you. It means you learn how to wake up on difficult days and still choose life. It means discovering that your heart can hold sorrow and gratitude at the same time.

What we face, we can heal from.

What we process, we can integrate.

What we avoid, we remain bound to.

If you are willing to face your grief by sitting with it, speaking about it, and praying through it, healing will come. Usually not all at once, and definitely not on your timetable, but it will sure happen gradually, steadily, faithfully, and deeply. And one day, you will wake up, just as I did and realise that while the loss remains, peace has quietly taken its place beside it.

That is the work of healing.

Chapter 9

WHEN DO I SEEK ADDITIONAL HELP?

I have heard many people's grief stories, but one that has had a profound impact on me is that of my friend, author and leadership coach, Marian Favors. Her story left me wondering, "How much grief can one person take?"

For Marian, grief was not just a one-off experience, or an experience that came evenly spaced but rather, it came in waves that were relentless, overlapping, and often timed cruelly close to moments meant for celebration.

For nearly five years, death followed her family, often circling the holidays as if grief itself had marked the calendar. It began with the loss of her brother. Then came two nephews, both only twenty-seven years old and taken suddenly, violently, and far too soon. One was shot while simply visiting his girlfriend, caught in the crossfire of a world that mistook him for someone else. The other died from a drug overdose after Marian had tried desperately to bring him home, sensing something was wrong, and hoping intervention might change the ending.

But nothing prepared her for Christmas Day, 2021! Around nine o'clock that morning, Marian received a phone call that her dad who lived in Arkansas, United States had died. While she was still trying to process the news, another phone call came in two hours later that her forty-three-year-old son who lived in California had also died. Can you imagine losing both your son and Dad on the same day? On Christmas day! Two lives. Two goodbyes. One heart left to hold both.

She remembers wondering how anyone is supposed to grieve two people at once. We talk about multitasking, she says, but grief doesn't work that way. You don't divide your pain evenly. One loss inevitably rises to the surface, demanding your breath, your attention, your tears. For Marian, that loss was her son. He was her child. He was young. And his death shattered her in ways that no amount of faith or forewarning could have prepared her for. He died of a heart attack, leaving five children behind.

Her father's death carried a different weight. He was ninety. Dementia had already taken him years before his body followed. Marian had grieved him slowly, quietly, long before the actual death. She had already said goodbye in a thousand small ways like when he stopped speaking, when he no longer knew her, when caring for him became a full act of devotion. His passing felt like release from the heart-breaking state that dementia had put him, even though it was still very painful to lose him.

Grief, Marian learned, does not completely disappear, even with the passage of time. It simply changes form. It shows up when she celebrates her grandchildren's birthdays and realises their father is missing. It appears when she imagines a future that will never happen, like her son walking his daughter down the aisle, laughing beside her in moments that now live only in imagination. There will always be thoughts of what could have been.

And then there was the death of her mother, who suddenly died just one year after the death of her son and Dad. This was just a day before a planned visit, and it was devastating to say the least.

Another death which Marian acknowledged that she had never talked about openly was the death of her daughter at birth. It was stillborn, carrying her child for nine months, only to be delivered without a cry. This loss so profound that it took years for her to come to a place of acceptance.

Each death carried its own sting. Each demanded something different from her heart. But one truth remained consistent: Marian did what many grieving people do. She kept going. After her son died on Christmas Day, she returned to work the very next week. Not because she was okay but because sitting still meant thinking, and thinking meant feeling. Work became her refuge. Productivity became her shield. From the outside, she looked strong, capable and resilient. But inside, something was quietly unraveling. Her energy was fast disappearing. Rest, something her children had never seen her do, became unavoidable. Food lost its appeal. Exhaustion followed her everywhere. Even though she felt she was still functioning, she knew this was not the way to live. It wasn't until she sat with a therapist and spoke the words out loud, "I'm not hungry. I'm tired. I don't want to get out of bed," that she heard the truth reflected back to her.

"You're depressed," the therapist told her.

Clinical depression, and this is a normal response to overwhelming grief that is not processed.

Marian had reached a point many grieving people get to, without realising it. The place where strength alone is no longer enough, a place where support is not optional but mandatory.

Her healing did not begin when the grief ended, it began when she allowed herself to be helped.

****

Although the depth of Marian's losses is profound, her reaction to grief is not unusual. Many people experiencing grief continue to show up, keep working, and care for others long after their inner resources have been depleted. From the outside, they appear to be strong and coping well but inside, they are slowly shutting down. At this point, grief moves from something we are carrying to something to something carrying us under. And this is when it becomes crucial to seek help.

Knowing when to seek additional help is not about weakness but about awareness and wisdom. I am glad that Marian recognised this and sought the necessary help.

> *Knowing when to seek additional help is not about weakness but about wisdom.*

SIGNS THAT EXTRA SUPPORT MAY BE HELPFUL

Grief expresses itself in many ways with each person having a different experience. Yet there are moments when grief begins to signal that more support could be helpful, not because you are weak or something is wrong with you, but because the grief has become too heavy and taken root.

Below are some of the signs that indicate that you may need some extra support when grieving. Remember that these are signs, and I am just naming experiences not diagnosing. They are invitations to pause, notice, and respond with care.

Emotional Signs

One of the most common signals is emotional numbness. Instead of intense sadness, grief may show up as emptiness, a sense of going through the motions without feeling fully present. You may notice that joy, excitement, or even sorrow feels muted, as though life is happening behind a pane of glass. For some, this numbness is paired with a quiet hopelessness, a feeling that things will never truly feel better, even if you can't explain why.

Another emotional signal is persistent guilt, shame, or self-blame. These feelings may circle endlessly, replaying moments from the past: If only I had noticed sooner... If only I had said something different... If only I had done more. While some guilt is a common part of grief, it becomes toxic when it refuses to loosen its grip. When it colours your sense of self and convinces you that you are somehow responsible for the loss or its outcome.

Grief can also feel overwhelming when you become stuck in a single emotional state with little relief. This might look like constant sadness, ongoing anger, or unrelenting anxiety. The emotions themselves are not the problem, it is the absence of movement, the feeling that nothing shifts no matter how much time passes or how hard you try.

Physical and Behavioural Signs

Grief does not stay confined to the heart. It often settles into the body. Ongoing sleep disruption, exhaustion, or panic symptoms are common signals that grief is taking a physical toll. You may struggle to fall asleep or wake frequently throughout the night. You may feel deeply tired even after rest, or experience sudden waves of anxiety such as racing thoughts, tightness in the chest, or shortness of breath even without an obvious trigger.

Another sign is using coping behaviours to avoid feeling. Some people throw themselves into work, staying constantly busy to outrun their thoughts. We saw this with Marian when she returned to work just days after burying her son, not because she was ready, but because being still felt unbearable. Work gave her structure. It gave her something to focus on besides the ache she already carried with her.

Others turn to food, alcohol, relentless scrolling on the phone, or self-isolation, not because they enjoy it, but because it helps them to numb the pain. These behaviours are understandable attempts to survive pain, but when they become the primary way you cope, they can quietly deepen suffering.

Grief may also interfere with basic daily care. You might forget to eat, avoid medical appointments, let responsibilities pile up, or struggle to complete tasks that once felt manageable. These are all signs that your emotional load has exceeded your capacity to cope with the situation.

Relational Signs

Grief can be profoundly isolating, even when you are surrounded by people. One signal that additional support may be needed is withdrawing from others or feeling unable to connect, even with those you trust. You may cancel plans repeatedly, stop returning messages, or feel drained by conversation. Sometimes it's not that you don't want company, rather, it's that you don't have the energy to explain yourself or hold space for anyone else.

Another relational sign is feeling misunderstood or invisible, even when support is offered. Friends may say the "right" things, but nothing seems to land. You may feel unseen in your pain or pressured to move forward before you're ready. This disconnect can leave you feeling more alone than before.

Grief can also surface as increased irritability or emotional outbursts. You may find yourself snapping at loved ones, feeling easily overwhelmed, or reacting strongly to small frustrations. Often, these moments are not about anger at others but are signs of emotional exhaustion and unmet needs.

Safety-Related Signs

There are moments when grief moves beyond deep sorrow and begins to affect a person's sense of safety. These moments can be frightening, not only because of the thoughts themselves, but because many people feel ashamed or afraid to admit they are having them.

If you recognise yourself in any of the experiences below, it does not mean you want to die. More often, it means you are overwhelmed, exhausted, and in need of care so please seek help immediately.

One safety-related sign is thoughts of wanting to disappear. When you begin to have thoughts like, "I just want it all to stop. I wish I could go to sleep and not wake up. I want to vanish for a while." Even though these thoughts are not as much as about death as they are about relief (relief from pain, from responsibility, from the weight of grief that feels unending), immediate help should be sought.

Another sign is a sense that life no longer has meaning. Grief can strip away purpose, identity, and hope. You may find yourself questioning why you're still here, what you are living for, or whether anything ahead matters anymore. This loss of meaning can feel especially confusing if you were once grounded in faith, family, or a strong sense of direction. When the future feels empty or pointless, it is a signal that grief has reached a depth that deserves immediate attention and support.

A particularly important sign is feeling unsafe with your own thoughts. This might look like intrusive or frightening ideas that come uninvited, thoughts that spiral quickly, or moments when you worry about what your mind might do when you're alone. You may feel afraid to sit in silence or uneasy trusting yourself late at night. This is not a failure of faith, strength, or character but often a sign of emotional overload and nervous system distress.

These experiences are common in profound grief, but they should never be faced alone.

If you are having thoughts that scare you, or if you feel unsure about your safety, reaching out is not optional self-care but an act of protection. This might mean contacting a trusted person, a therapist, a faith leader, or a crisis support service. Help at this stage is not about fixing the grief but about keeping you safe while you grieve.

Grief can convince us that silence is safer than speaking, but that is totally a lie. Naming these thoughts, out loud, with someone trained or trusted can reduce their power and create space for hope to re-enter, even slowly.

If you are in immediate danger or feel unable to keep yourself safe, seek emergency help right away. You are not a burden. Your life has value, even when grief makes it hard to feel.

> *You are not a burden. Your life has value, even when grief makes it hard to feel.*

A Gentle Reframe

Experiencing these signs does not mean you are grieving incorrectly. It means your grief is asking for more care, more space, and possibly more support than you can provide on your own.

Strength is not measured by how much pain you endure silently. Sometimes, the strongest response to grief is recognising when it's time to invite someone else into the work of healing. Don't wait until you are in crisis to seek help. Grief does not require a breaking point to deserve support, and you don't have to suffer in ways that you don't have.

WHAT TO DO NEXT

Recognising these signs can be unsettling for some because it stirs fear or resistance that makes them wonder, "Does this mean something is wrong with me?" While for others, it is relieving because it now gives language for what they are experiencing.

Awareness is not a diagnosis. It is a doorway. When you notice any of these signals, the next step is not to judge yourself but simply to respond with care. You do not need to know exactly what kind of help you need. You only need to acknowledge the truth that I don't have to carry this alone.

For some, the next step is saying the words out loud for the first time, I'm not okay, I need help. For others, it may mean reaching out to a trusted person and asking for help on how to find support, rather than trying to figure out everything by yourself. While for others, it may mean directly contacting a therapist, a grief counselor, a medical professional, a faith leader or calling a crisis line especially when your thoughts feel unmanageable.

> *There is no single "right" way forward. What matters is movement, however small, toward care.*

There is no single "right" way forward. What matters is movement, however small, toward care. You do not have to be ready for healing to begin. You only have to be willing to be supported.

In the next section, we will explore what support can look like, and how to ask for it without shame.

WHAT SUPPORT CAN LOOK LIKE

When people hear the phrase "seeking help," the only option they often imagine is therapy, with the assumption that something is seriously wrong. In reality, support comes in many forms, and the right kind of help often depends on where you are in your grief, what feels safest, and what is most accessible to you right now.

Support is not one-size-fits-all. It is layered, flexible, and allowed to change over time.

Professional Therapy and Grief Counseling

Therapists and grief counselors provide a confidential space where grief does not have to be minimized, explained away, or rushed. Therapy can help you explore complex emotions such as guilt, anger, numbness, trauma, or depression, and identify when grief has become intertwined with anxiety, clinical depression, or past wounds.

For some people, therapy is short-term: a place to process a specific loss. For others, it becomes longer-term support as grief unfolds and intersects with identity, relationships, and mental health. Therapy is not about "fixing" the grief but about helping you understand and process it with greater support.

Grief Coaching

Grief coaching offers a different but equally meaningful kind of support. While therapy often focuses on diagnosis, mental health, and emotional processing, grief coaching is typically more forward-facing and practical, helping people navigate life with grief rather than trying to move past it.

A grief coach may help you:

- Make sense of where you are in your grief journey
- Identify what feels hardest right now and why
- Develop coping strategies for daily life, work, and relationships
- Rebuild routines, confidence, and a sense of purpose
- Learn how to carry grief without being consumed by it

Grief coaching can be especially helpful for those who feel functional but overwhelmed. Those who are feeling lost, exhausted, or stuck inside. It can also support people who have completed therapy and are asking, how do I live now?

Coaching does not replace therapy or medical care when those are needed. Instead, it often works alongside them, offering structure, encouragement, and accountability as you learn to live forward after loss.

Support Groups

Grief groups offer something uniquely powerful: the reminder that you are not alone. Sitting with others who have experienced similar losses can ease the sense of isolation that grief often creates. You may hear your own thoughts spoken out loud by someone else for the first time, and that will make you feel understood without having to explain.

Support groups may be general or loss-specific (such as for parents, widows, siblings, or sudden loss). Some people speak often; others listen quietly for weeks before sharing. Both are valid. Healing does not require performance.

Faith-Based or Spiritual Support

For many people, faith is a source of comfort during grief. Spiritual leaders, pastors, chaplains, or trusted mentors can offer prayer, perspective, and companionship that honours both sorrow and hope.

Faith-based support does not require having all the answers or even feeling strong in belief. Doubt, anger, and confusion are not signs of lack of faith, but they are often part of honest grief.

The right spiritual support makes room for questions, lament, and truth. It doesn't silence pain but walks with you through it.

> *The right spiritual support makes room for questions, lament, and truth. It doesn't silence pain but walks with you through it.*

Medical Care

Sometimes grief affects the body in ways that require medical attention. Persistent insomnia, panic attacks, extreme fatigue, loss of appetite, or symptoms of depression may benefit from evaluation by a primary health care provider or psychiatrist.

Medical care does not replace emotional or spiritual support, but it can be an important part of stabilizing the body so healing can continue. Accepting medical help is recognising that grief is not only emotional but also physiological.

Trusted People with Clear Boundaries

Not all support has to be formal. A trusted friend, family member, or mentor can offer meaningful care, especially when expectations are clear. This might be someone who listens without trying to fix, someone who can sit with silence, or someone who helps with practical needs when energy is low.

The goal is not to have many people involved, but to have safe people, those who respect your pace and honour your experience.

HOW TO ASK FOR SUPPORT WITHOUT SHAME

Asking for help can feel harder than grief itself. Many people worry about being a burden, saying the wrong thing, or falling apart once they start talking. These fears are common, and understandable.

You do not need to justify your pain to deserve support.

You do not need to justify your pain to deserve support.

Start small. You don't have to tell the whole story. One honest sentence is enough. You can say things like:

- "I'm not doing as well as I look."
- "I'm struggling more than I expected."
- "I need help, and I don't know what kind yet."

If words feel heavy, ask for help with the logistics:

- "Can you help me find a therapist or support group?"
- "Can you sit with me while I make this call?"
- "Can you check in on me this week?"

If reaching out to a professionals or support group, you could say something like this to start the conversation.

"Hello, I found your contact information for bereavement support. I'm currently grieving and would like to know what services you offer and how I might get started."

If shame rises, as it often does, remind yourself that needing help is not sign of failure but evidence of wisdom in knowing your limits as a human being. Even the strongest people reach limits, and the most resilient hearts need reinforcement after deep loss. You are allowed to borrow strength when yours feels thin.

Asking for support does not mean you are giving up control. It means you are choosing not to face grief alone. And sometimes, that choice becomes the turning point, the moment healing begins to feel possible again.

CHOOSING SUPPORT AS AN ACT OF RESILIENCE

Resilience is often misunderstood. We picture it as strength without strain, perseverance without pause, survival without support. But grief teaches us a different truth. Resilience is not measured by how much pain you can carry alone. It is revealed in how you respond when the weight becomes too heavy.

Seeking help does not mean grief has overcome you. It means you have recognised your limits and honoured them. It means you have listened to the signals of your heart, your body, and your spirit, and chosen care instead of silence.

Marian's story reminds us that grief can coexist with productivity, faith, and responsibility, and still quietly deplete us. She did not lack strength. But even as a strong woman, she reached a place where strength alone was no longer enough. Her resilience showed up not in pushing harder, but in pausing, asking for help, and allowing others to walk with her.

There is no prize for carrying grief alone. There is only the cost of doing so. Resilience after loss is about becoming someone who knows when to reach for support, when to rest, and when to let healing take the lead. It is about learning to live forward with grief—not in denial of it and not buried beneath it.

If this chapter has helped you recognise signs you've been ignoring, let that awareness be a beginning, not a verdict. You can start today. And you will realise that help-seeking is not the opposite of resilience. Rather, it is one of its most powerful expressions.

So, whether your next step is a conversation, a phone call, a moment of prayer, or simply the decision not to do this alone anymore, know this: choosing support is choosing life. It is choosing hope, even when hope feels fragile. Reaching out for support is a courageous step. You deserve compassion, understanding, and care as you navigate your grief.

You can do this.

See appendix for a list of where to get support.

NOTE ON CHOOSING SUPPORT

Support does not have to be perfect to be *helpful*, and it doesn't have to be permanent. What matters is that a person feels safe, heard, and respected in the space they choose.

Starting small is okay. Trying something and realising it's not the right fit is okay. You can stop it and try other options until you get what is the right fit for you. Asking for help is not the end, it's a beginning.

Chapter 10
HOW DO I MOVE FORWARD WITH LOVE?

My daughter Grace taught me unconditional love. From the moment she entered the world, nothing about our journey looked ordinary, but everything about it was meaningful. In spite her severe disabilities, a rare condition known as Cornelia de Lang syndrome, Grace lived for fifteen years. Fifteen years in which she taught me patience when I needed it most, compassion I didn't know I was capable of, and a kind of love that asks for nothing in return. Loving Grace required presence, tenderness, and resilience. It also quietly reshaped who I was becoming.

When Grace died, the pain was immense. Losing a child breaks something open in you that never fully closes again. But over time, I came to understand something vital: while I could not stop the pain of losing her, I could choose what I carried forward. We are not meant to carry raw pain forever; we are meant to carry love.

Living in Ireland, where Grace was born, and later in the UK, where she eventually died, I saw firsthand the support available for children with disabilities and their families. That support made our journey survivable. It also made me aware of a painful truth that many families in Africa have no such help. The compassion and unconditional love Grace cultivated in me could not remain idle. It needed somewhere to go.

That is how the Grace Miracle Ehigocho (GME) Foundation was born. Through it, we support children living with disabilities across Africa by providing mobility aids like wheelchairs and access to medical care. Every child we reach carries a piece of Grace's legacy forward. No one gets to choose their experiences. But everyone gets to choose what they do with them.

No one gets to choose their experiences. But everyone gets to choose what they do with them.

Today, when I see the joyful smiles of the children our foundation supports, I see Grace. Not in pain, but in motion. Not in loss, but in love, continuing to live through us. I am profoundly grateful for the fifteen years I shared with my beautiful daughter. Grace is no longer here in the way I wish she were, but her love is still at work in the world.

****

Grace's legacy lives through a foundation but that is only my expression of carrying love forward. Your path may be different. Not everyone will start a charity. Not everyone will turn grief into visible action. And not everyone is ready to do anything at all. What matters is not what you do with your grief, but what you choose to carry.

Pain demands energy. It tightens the body, clouds the mind, and asks questions like "Why me?" that makes us feel like victims and keeps us tethered to the moment of loss. Love, on the other hand, expands. It asks better questions like: What did this person give me? What did loving them awaken in me? How might that love continue to move through my life?

Carrying love forward does not mean denying pain. It means refusing to let pain be the heaviest thing that you carry. Love can go with you too.

HOW TO CARRY LOVE FORWARD (NOT PAIN)

Carrying love forward instead of pain is a choice, and it is a choice everyone can make. It does not mean denying grief or pretending that loss did not change you. It means deciding, over time, what will shape your life more deeply: the wound of loss, or the love that existed before it.

So, here are your invitations to make that choice.

1. Separate Love from Suffering

In grief, love and suffering often feel inseparable. The intensity of pain can make us believe that hurting is proof of how deeply we loved. But suffering is not love's currency, it is love's aftershock. It is our human reaction to the blow that death has dealt us, not the relationship itself.

Long before loss entered your life, love already existed. We feel pain because love matters. The pain you carry is not the measure of your love; it is the wound created when someone or something precious is gone. Grief research and attachment theory remind us that pain is the nervous system struggling to adjust to absence and not love increasing in value through suffering.

To begin carrying love forward, gently ask yourself:

- What parts of my grief are expressions of love?
- What parts are my nervous system in survival mode?

You may notice that the parts rooted in survival which shows up as hypervigilance, replaying the moment of loss, and constant emotional flooding, are what keep you in prolonged suffering.

Separating love from suffering does not mean you erase the pain or just forget the deceased. It is shifting from a state of acute, all-encompassing agony to a place where cherished memories can coexist with daily life.

You may have heard the quote attributed to Haruki Murakami that says, "Pain is inevitable. Suffering is optional." In grief, this means suffering is not the only place you should live. You can gradually and gently move to a place where love leads. Suffering asks us to keep reliving the moment of loss. Love invites us to remember the relationship.

2. Identify What Love Gave You

Loss ends a life, but it does not end a relationship. Relationships continue through what they leave behind in us. Rather than focusing only on what was taken, I invite you to look toward what was received by asking yourself:

- What did loving them teach me?
- What qualities did they draw out of me?
- Who am I because they existed?

In answering these questions honestly, you may discover capacities such as patience, courage, tenderness, and endurance that you developed because of this relationship. You may recognise values that took root in you quietly over time because of the relationship. And you may also notice how your identity has been shaped by loving them.

Raising Grace required a kind of love that was patient, embodied, and unconditional. Loving her trained my heart in compassion long before I knew how deeply I would need it later. When Grace died, that compassion did not disappear. It became part of who I am.

Loss can take a person or a dream from you, but it does not take what your relationship with them has built within you. That inheritance, those inner resources is what you can carry forward.

> *Loss can take a person or a dream from you, but it does not take what your relationship with them has built within you.*

3. Let Love Change Form

After loss, many people try to preserve love in its old form through routines, presence or familiar roles. When those are gone, it can feel as though love itself has disappeared. But love doesn't end or die when someone dies, it simply transforms.

Research into post-traumatic growth suggests that while loss can shatter assumptions about life, it can also enable us to grow as we allow love to evolve naturally over time.

For some, love may take the form of:

- Becoming more patient
- Advocating quietly for others
- Being gentler with yourself
- Living with deeper presence
- Becoming more creative
- Caring for others

- Quiet remembrance

For others, love becomes internal:

- A voice of reassurance
- A moral compass
- A source of strength in difficult moments

There is no "correct" expression of love. Love only asks to move. Holding on to suffering in the name of love freezes it, but allowing love to transform sets it free.

For me, love needed motion. Living in Ireland and later the UK, I experienced the support systems that helped Grace live with dignity. When I saw how little support existed for children with disabilities in Africa, love could not remain still. It became action. It became the Grace Miracle Ehigocho Foundation. Love changed shape, and in doing so, it kept Grace present in the world.

4. Release the Myth of "Moving On"

One of the heaviest expectations placed on grieving people is the idea that they must eventually "move on." This suggests forgetting, closing a chapter, and carrying on as though that part of life never existed. If that is what moving on means, then it implies that love has an expiration date.

But no one really moves on from love. You move forward with it. Moving forward with love after grief means:

- Carrying memories without being consumed by them
- Allowing joy to coexist with sorrow

- Letting life grow around what was lost

Grief researchers and clinicians now emphasize integration, not closure. We don't leave love behind; we learn how to carry it differently.

I move forward with love from Grace's life into the lives of children whose mobility has been restored, into the tenderness I now bring into spaces of suffering, and into the knowing that love can outlive loss.

5. Choose Meaning at Your Own Pace

There is often unspoken pressure to "do something meaningful" with grief by turning your pain into purpose quickly, visibly, and admirably. But you must remember this: meaning-making cannot be rushed.

In the early stages of grief, survival must be your priority. You need to stay alive before you can make meaning. Grief unfolds in seasons, and each season asks for something different. One season may require endurance. Another may require rest. Another may finally make space for purpose.

The choice to carry love forward does not demand immediacy. It requires honesty. Love moves when the body and soul are ready. I did not create Grace's legacy while I was drowning in loss. It emerged gradually, as compassion ripened into clarity. Love waited until I could walk again.

Meaning does not demand urgency. There is no deadline for transformation. Love is patient.

6. Allow Love to Outlast Pain

You will realise that pain is loud, but it is temporary. Love on the other hand is quieter but enduring. When you begin to trust that love is stronger than the pain of your loss, you will notice something subtle: love evolves into a force that outlasts pain.

Pain marks where love was wounded. But love marks where life can still grow. You don't carry love forward by forcing yourself to feel better. You carry it forward by letting love to shape how you live, how you see others, and how gently you hold yourself.

RITUALS THAT CARRY LOVE FORWARD

In grief, many people assume that remembrance must be heavy to be meaningful, and that honouring the dead requires reopening the wound again and again. But rituals are not meant to retraumatise us. They are meant to hold us.

Anthropologists have long observed that ritual is one of humanity's oldest tools for surviving loss. From communal mourning practices to anniversary remembrance, rituals help societies regulate emotion, mark transition, and restore a sense of order after death. Grief researchers echo this, showing that well-chosen rituals can help the nervous system feel safe again by giving grief a container, a place to go, rather than letting it spill everywhere.

The purpose of ritual is not to preserve pain. It is to give love a place to rest and reappear.

Rituals that carry love forward are not grand or performative. They are often quiet, repeatable, and flexible. They meet us where we are, rather than where we think we should be.

Gentle Principles for Grief Rituals

Before choosing or creating a ritual, it helps to hold a few truths:

- A ritual should comfort, not exhaust you
- You are allowed to change or stop a ritual at any time
- A ritual can be private and still be powerful
- Love does not require suffering for it to be honoured

If a ritual leaves you emotionally flooded, depleted, or stuck in the moment of loss, it may be asking too much of you right now, and you can skip it. That does not mean you love any less. It means your wellbeing is important, and you need to be in a good place to express love.

Rituals of Time and Containment

One of the reasons grief becomes overwhelming is that it has no boundaries. It appears uninvited, in places or situations we least expect. It could show up supermarkets, at traffic lights, or even in ordinary conversations. Rituals help contain grief without suppressing it.

Grief researchers such as Dennis Klass and Margaret Stroebe have shown that intentional remembrance, especially when it is time-bound helps mourners stay connected without being consumed. These rituals gently signal to the nervous system: There will be space for this.

In our family, we honour Grace in this way. Each year on her birthday and on the anniversary of her death, we come together. We visit her graveside with flowers, and sometimes balloons. We intentionally remember her and the value she has added to our lives. And then, importantly, we go for a meal together. That meal is not an afterthought; it is part of our ritual. It reminds us that Grace's life was not only about loss. It was about love, laughter, presence, and connection. We grieve her absence, but we also celebrate that she lived. Grief is acknowledged, but it does not get the final word.

This kind of ritual allows grief to be honoured without overwhelming daily life. It creates a rhythm: remembrance and return.

Rituals of Presence

Some days, especially in early grief, even structured rituals feel like too much. On those days, presence is enough.

Gentle rituals of presence may include:

- Lighting a candle and sitting quietly for a few minutes
- Speaking their name softly, without expectation of emotion
- Placing a hand on your heart and remembering one loving moment
- Carrying a small object that reminds you of them

These rituals do not ask you to relive the moment of loss. They simply acknowledge the bond. They say: You mattered, and you still matter.

Anthropologist Victor Turner described ritual as a way of creating meaning during liminal times, periods when life feels suspended between what was and what will be. Grief is one of those times. Presence-based rituals help us stay grounded when the world feels unfamiliar.

Rituals of Continuation

As grief evolves, many people feel drawn toward rituals that allow love to move beyond memory and into action. This aligns with what grief researchers call continuing bonds—the idea that maintaining a relationship with the deceased can be healthy, adaptive, and life-giving.

These rituals might include:

- Doing an act of kindness in their name

- Supporting a cause connected to what mattered to them
- Passing on a lesson they taught you
- Showing up for others with the compassion they cultivated in you

This is how Grace's love continues in my life. The compassion I learned through caring for her did not end with her death. It expanded into advocacy, into service, and into the Grace Miracle Ehigocho Foundation. Love changed form, but it did not lose its essence.

Rituals of continuation remind us that love is not static. It wants to move and this ritual let it move outward.

Rituals of Dialogue

Many people continue an inner dialogue with the person who has died. Even if you know that they may not hear you, it is still a way of feeling connected and it is deeply human.

You might:

- Speak to them during quiet moments
- Ask what they would want for you now
- Imagine their response when you are struggling

Grief researchers recognise this as a natural expression of continuing bonds. Love does not disappear when a body does. It learns how to speak differently.

A CLOSING INVITATION

Rituals are not about holding on to the past. They are about allowing love to move forward with you.

You are not required to remember loudly.

You are not required to remember painfully.

You are only invited, when you are ready, to remember lovingly.

Carry love forward in ways that nourish you.

And if you are in a season when even the gentlest ritual feels unbearable, it does not mean you are failing the person you loved. Love does not keep score.

Carrying love forward is not a single decision. It is a series of small, human choices made over time. Choices to soften instead of harden, to remember without drowning, to live in a way that allows love to outlast loss.

> *Grief does not have to be the heaviest thing you carry.*
> *Love can go with you, too*

Grief will always matter. But it does not have to be the heaviest thing you carry. Love can go with you, too.

CONCLUSION

I wrote this book by sharing parts of my own story, along with the real-life experiences of others, in the hope that somewhere in these pages you might recognise pieces of your own journey. I hope this book have brought you encouragement, hope, and perhaps a measure of healing as you continue moving forward.

If something in these pages has spoken to you, I would truly love to hear from you.

Before we part, I would like to leave you with this letter.

Dear Reader,

Thank you for making it to the end of the book. You have already done something remarkable.

You stayed.

You stayed with words that may have touched places still tender.

You stayed with memories you did not ask to revisit.

That takes courage, even if it does not feel like it.
I am not writing to you as someone who has figured out everything about grief. I am writing to you as someone who has lived inside it.

I know how loss can narrow our world.
How ordinary days can begin to feel unfamiliar.
How it can leave you unsure of who you are now.

If you feel changed, it's understandable.
If you feel tired, that makes sense too.

Because you are unique, the way you are grieving is also unique.

There is no correct pace.
No right expression.
No moment when you are meant to be "done."

Grief is not a task to complete.
It is love learning how to live with absence.

You do not have to carry pain forever in order to honour the one you lost. Pain may have arrived with grief, but love was there first. Love can gently lead now, in ways that do not overwhelm you.

Some days, carrying love forward will look like doing very little.
Some days it will look like rest.
Other days it may look like remembering, or laughing, or simply getting through the day.
All of it counts.

If joy finds you unexpectedly, you are allowed to receive it.
It does not erase what you have lost.
It means love is still present.

You do not need to leave anyone behind in order to keep living. Love can walk with you, quietly and faithfully into whatever comes next.

Thank you for trusting these pages.
Thank you for staying with yourself.

You are not alone as you go forward.
Love goes with you.
And wherever your next step leads, may you walk it with kindness toward yourself.

With love & care,
Eyum Ejiga

MEET THE AUTHOR

Eyum Ejiga is an inspirational author, speaker, and grief-informed Certified Coach dedicated to helping people overcome adversity, and move forward to live purposeful, fulfilling lives. Drawing from her own lived experience of loss and resilience, she guides individuals and organizations in transforming adversity into strength and meaning.

She is the CEO of EE-Bridging Solutions Limited, a coaching and training company focused on personal and leadership development, and the founder of My Pain Your Ministry International, a nonprofit organization that has impacted thousands of lives worldwide through empowerment, healing, and hope-centered initiatives.

Eyum holds a Bachelor of Science in Computer Science from the University of Benin, Nigeria, a Bachelor of Science (Honours) in Applied Accounting, and an MBA from Oxford Brookes University. Her academic background, combined with professional training and lived experience, shapes her practical, structured, and compassionate approach to personal growth and leadership development.

A sought-after international speaker, Eyum has shared powerful messages on global platforms, including the International Maxwell Conference, and continues to reach thousands weekly through her teachings on resilience, grief, leadership, and growth.

A recipient of several awards recognising her impact and leadership, Eyum is the author of four books. *Finding A Way Forward After Loss* reflects her calling to walk alongside others through loss, offering understanding, hope, and a path toward healing.

APPENDICES

FINDING SUPPORT FOR GRIEF

1. Therapy and Grief Counselling

United Kingdom

- NHS Talking Therapies – The NHS provides free access to counselling, Cognitive Behavioural Therapy (CBT), and other therapeutic support in many areas through self-referral. Visit website:

  https://www.nhs.uk/tests-and-treatments/talking-therapies/

- Cruse Bereavement Support – One of the UK's leading grief support charities, offering emotional support, helplines, counselling, and resources for people experiencing loss.

  Visit: https://www.cruse.org.uk/

- Mind (UK) – Provides information on mental health support, including local services and guidance on accessing help.

  Website: https://www.mind.org.uk/

International

• Psychology Today Therapist Directory – A global directory that allows you to search for therapists by location, specialty (including grief), and treatment approach. Visit: https://www.psychologytoday.com/us/therapists

2. Grief Coaching

Grief coaching is typically offered privately. To find a grief coach:

• Search online for "grief coach" or "bereavement coach" along with your city or country.
  Many coaches offer a free introductory call to explore whether the support feels like a good fit.

• Professional Coaching Directory
  o International Coaching Federation (ICF) – A global directory of credentialed coaches that allows filtering by specialty.
  Visit: https://coachingfederation.org/find-a-coach

3. Support Groups

Support groups provide a space to connect with others who understand the experience of loss.

United Kingdom

• Cruse Bereavement Support Groups – Offers both group and one-to-one support across the UK.
  Visit: https://www.cruse.org.uk/get-support

- The Good Grief Trust – A national hub providing a directory of bereavement services and community support across the UK.
  Visit: https://www.thegoodgrieftrust.org/
- Sands (Stillbirth & Neonatal Death Support) – Support for families affected by pregnancy loss or the death of a baby.
  Visit: https://www.sands.org.uk/

International / Online

- GriefShare – Provides grief recovery support groups and online communities around the world.
  Visit: https://www.griefshare.org/
- Many counsellors and organisations also offer virtual grief support groups via online platforms.

4. Faith-Based or Spiritual Support

For pastoral care and grief support, you can contact Local churches, mosques, synagogues, temples, and interfaith centres.

- Many religious organisations provide grief ministries, helplines, or chaplaincy services.
- Community clergy or chaplains may also offer home visits or one-to-one pastoral support.

5. Medical and Mental Health Support

United Kingdom

- GP Consultation – Your GP can help assess symptoms, provide guidance, and refer you to appropriate mental health services.
- NHS Urgent Mental Health Support – For urgent emotional distress or mental health crises.

Visit: https://www.nhs.uk/mental-health/get-urgent-help/

Pharmacists may also provide guidance on sleep support or advise when further medical care may be helpful.

6. Immediate Crisis Support

If you feel unsafe, overwhelmed, or concerned about your safety or thoughts, immediate help is available. These services are free and confidential.

United Kingdom

- Samaritans – 24/7 Emotional Support
  Visit: https://www.samaritans.org/
- NHS 111 – For urgent health support if you are unsure where to turn.

International

- Befrienders Worldwide – Crisis support helplines available in over 200 countries.
  Visit: https://www.befrienders.org/
- International Association for Suicide Prevention (IASP) – Directory of crisis centres by country.
  Visit:

https://www.iasp.info/resources/Crisis_Centres/

If someone is in immediate danger, contact local emergency services.

Online Search Suggestions

- "Grief support near me"
- "Therapist specialising in grief near me"
- "Bereavement helpline [your country]"

NOTES

1. Bowlby, J. (1980). Attachment and loss: Vol. 3. Loss: sadness and depression. Basic Books.

2. Brown, B. (2007). I thought it was just me (but it isn't): Telling the truth about perfectionism, inadequacy, and power. Gotham Books.

3. Burns, L. (2020, July 3). Elisabeth Kübler-Ross: The rise and fall of the five stages of grief. BBC News. Retrieved October 31, 2025, from https://www.bbc.co.uk/news/stories-53267505

4. Fenix, J. B., Cherlin, E. J., Prigerson, H. G., Johnson-Hurzeler, R., & Kasl, S. V. (2006). Religiousness and major depression among bereaved family caregivers: A 13-month follow-up study. Journal of Palliative Care, 22(4), 286–292.

5. Gillette H., & Silva S. (2021). 6 Coping Skills to Work Through Grief. Retrieved January 31, 2026, from https://psychcentral.com/health/coping-skills-for-grief

6. Goffman, E. (1963). Stigma: Notes on the management of spoiled identity. Prentice-Hall.

7. Gregory, C. (2021). How do I move on after a loss? The Loss Therapist. Retrieved August 31, 2025, from https://www.thelosstherapist.co.uk/blog/moving-on-from-loss

8. Khosravi, M. (2021). Worden's task-based approach for supporting people bereaved by COVID-19. Current Psychology. Retrieved November 5, 2025, from https://pmc.ncbi.nlm.nih.gov/articles/PMC7778565/

9. Klass, D., Silverman, P. R., & Nickman, S. L. (1996). Continuing bonds: New understandings of grief. Taylor & Francis.

10. Kübler-Ross, E. (1969). On death and dying. Macmillan.

11. Lewis, M. (2000). Self-conscious emotions: Embarrassment, pride, shame, and guilt. In M. Lewis & J. M. Haviland-Jones (Eds.), Handbook of emotions (2nd ed.). Guilford Press.

12. Lewis, M. (2019). The self-conscious emotions and the role of shame in psychopathology. In Handbook of emotional development. Springer.

13. Lewis, M., & Minar, N. (2022). Self-recognition and emotional knowledge. European Journal of Developmental Psychology.

14. Mind. (n.d.). Depression. Mind. Retrieved October 31, 2025, from https://www.mind.org.uk/information-support/types-of-mental-health-problems/depression/about-depression/

15. Neff, K. D. (2003). Self-compassion: An alternative conceptualization of a healthy attitude toward oneself. Self and Identity, 2(2), 85–101.

16. Neimeyer, R. A. (2001). Meaning reconstruction and the experience of loss. American Psychological Association.

17. Okoye, U. (2012). Widowhood, cultural practices and social justice in Nigeria. Journal of Social Development in Africa, 27(2), 57–84.

18. Oliver-Pyatt, W. (n.d.). The evolution of shame: Origin, understanding, and healing. Within Health. Retrieved January 18, 2026, from https://withinhealth.com/learn/within-summit-series/the-evolution-of-shame-origin-understanding-and-healing

19. Parkes, C. M. (1998). Bereavement: Studies of grief in adult life. Routledge.

20. Rosenblatt, P. C. (2008). Grief across cultures. Routledge.

21. Schwartzberg, S. S., & Janoff-Bulman, R. (1991). Grief and the search for meaning: Exploring the

assumptive worlds of bereaved college students. Journal of Social and Clinical Psychology, 10, 270–288.

22. Sherkat, D. E., & Reed, M. D. (1992). The effects of religion and social support on self-esteem and depression among the suddenly bereaved. Social Indicators Research, 26, 259–275.

23. Stroebe, M., & Schut, H. (1999). The dual process model of coping with bereavement: Rationale and description. Death Studies, 23(3), 197–224.

24. Stroebe, M., Schut, H., & Boerner, K. (2017). Cautioning health-care professionals: Bereaved persons are misguided through the stages of grief. Omega: Journal of Death and Dying, 74(4), 455–473.

25. Tangney, J. P., & Dearing, R. L. (2002). Shame and guilt. Guilford Press.

26. The Holy Bible, King James Version. (n.d.). Proverbs 17:22.

27. The Holy Bible, New International Version. (n.d.). Genesis 2:25.

28. The Holy Bible, New International Version. (n.d.). Genesis 3:7.

29. The Holy Bible, New International Version. (n.d.). Matthew 11:28-29.

30. Tomkins, S. S. (1963). Affect, imagery, consciousness: Vol. II. The negative affects. Springer.

31. Turner, V. (1969). The ritual process: Structure and anti-structure. Aldine Publishing.

32. Verywell Health. (n.d.-a). Autonomic nervous system anatomy. Retrieved January 15, 2026, from

https://www.verywellhealth.com/autonomic-nervous-system-anatomy-2488639

33. Verywell Health. (n.d.-b). Coping mechanisms. Retrieved January 31, 2026, from https://www.verywellhealth.com/coping-mechanisms-5272135

34. Worden, J. W. (2009). Grief counselling and grief therapy: A handbook for the mental health practitioner (4th ed.). Springer.

35. Worden, J. W. (2018). Grief counselling and grief therapy. Springer Publishing.

Disclaimer:

Online sources were accurate at the time of access but may change or be removed in the future.

Contact

For more information about Eyum, to book her to speak at your event, or to order any of her books (digital or hard copy), please visit:

www.amazon.com
https://ee-bridging-solutions.co.uk
www.mypainyourgainministries.com

To contact or connect with her:

Email: eyum@ee-bridging-solutions.co.uk
        eyumejiga@gmail.com

Social media @Eyum Ejiga
On LinkedIn, Facebook, Instagram & YouTube

Other Books by Eyum Ejiga

In this inspirational book, Eyum shares the story of the shock, pain, and trauma she experienced following the birth of her daughter, Grace, and the journey she took to find comfort and healing.

He Gave Me Comfort is a captivating story of a mother's faith, resilience, and hope. It is a book you will not want to put down until the very last page. Through her heartfelt testimony, Eyum reminds readers that even in life's most difficult moments, comfort and strength can be found. This powerful story will not only bring encouragement but also restore hope, whatever circumstances you may be facing, and inspire you to reach even greater heights. It is truly a must-read.

The wind howled fiercely as the storm raged on, its thunderous roar echoing like a lion deprived of its prey. Lightning split the darkened sky while violent gusts shook everything in their path. Gripped with fear, Ihotu wondered, "Is this merely a thunderstorm, or something far more destructive—a hurricane or a tornado?"

As the storm intensified, Ihotu found herself reflecting on the many storms she had faced throughout her life. Each flash of lightning and crash of thunder reminded her of the challenges, trials, and uncertainties that had shaped her journey from childhood into early adulthood.

Through the Storm is a powerful and gripping story of resilience, courage, and hope. It follows a young girl's journey through the many challenges—life's inevitable storms—that test her strength and faith. Through her experiences, readers will discover practical lessons about perseverance, growth, and finding the courage to move forward even in the midst of life's fiercest storms.

Both inspiring and deeply moving, this story will encourage, inform, and entertain readers while reminding them that no storm lasts forever.

"Mama Grace!" For some, it is simply a name; for others, it is a title that conveys respect. But for Eyum, it became something much deeper; a life-changing revelation.

Through the privilege of nurturing her daughter, Grace, Eyum came to discover not only the meaning of grace but how to live it daily. What began as a simple expression of motherhood unfolded into a profound spiritual insight about the power of grace in every area of life.

In Mama Grace, Eyum shares these powerful lessons and practical truths with readers. If you are going through a difficult season and wondering how you will make it through, this book offers encouragement and guidance. It reveals how grace can carry you from where you are to where you desire to be.

You will discover that there is a dimension of grace available for every challenge, every season, and every aspect of your life. And you will learn how to receive and walk in that grace.